50 LAWS OF LIFE

Perfect Justice through Divine Law

FRED M. MOSELY

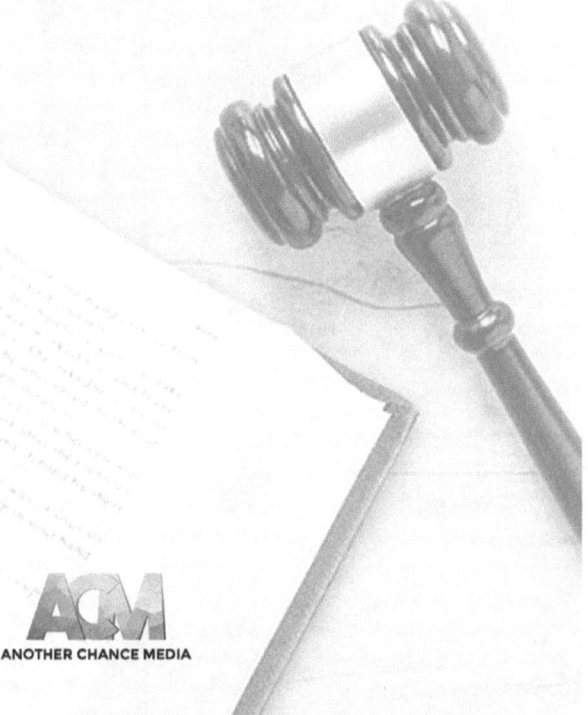

ANOTHER CHANCE MEDIA

50 LAWS OF LIFE

Copyright © 2020 by Fred Mosely

All rights reserved. Printed in the United States of America. No part of this work may be reproduced or transmitted in any form or by any means without the written permission from the publishing company.

For information contact:
Another Chance Media
anotherchanceglobalmedia.org

Book and cover design by
Another Chance Global Media

ISBN #9781732520530
Second Edition: September 2023

Dear Reader,

This introductory book to the 50 Laws of Life is to give the very basic concept of the Laws of Life and is not a comprehensive study. It is written in such a way that every reader will be able to understand. I want the meaning of each law to be clear and allow you to begin to think about how each plays out in our everyday lives.

A law is a Law of Life on the basis that it is written in the Bible as an absolute, there is scripture in the Old and New Testament to support it, and it is consistent throughout the Bible.

I hope that this book will spur you to further the study of the Laws of Life.

Yours in Christ,

Fred Mosely

DEDICATION

This book is dedicated to Almighty God who through His Spirit has entrusted me with the invaluable truths contained in the Laws of Life and with the responsibility of sharing these laws with the Body of Christ and whosoever will.

PREFACE

About Justice Ministries International

Justice Ministries International, is a not-for-profit entity, established by Fred M. Mosely in the hope of helping society to avoid the pathetic and futile search for justice in all the wrong places. Many people, believers and unbelievers inclusive, obviously hold to the opinion that there is no justice in the world. That may very well be true as it relates to man's justice, but not God's. Man may believe that his laws are paramount, but having practiced man's laws and studied God's Law's extensively, Fred Mosely comes to the conclusion that God's Laws obviously supersede all of the Laws of Man.

Justice Ministries International is therefore here to proclaim the Justice of God. True justice comes only from God. Yes, God is love. God is the truth. God is righteousness, God is peace and God is mercy; these are some of the many attributes of God; but also God is a God of justice, perfect justice. The human mind is too limited to conceive of the absolute and perfect justice of God.

INTRODUCTION

This book is an expansion to the introduction of a God inspired series of teachings in simplified format on the truth that perfect justice can be obtained only through Spiritual Laws, referred to herein as the Laws of Life. This inspiration was given to Fred M. Mosely who holds the Juris Doctor and Master of Laws Degrees, which he has practiced as a federal and state prosecutor, defense attorney and judge. Above all, the author desires to be known as a Christian who received Divine Inspiration to teach the world the essence and benefits of The Laws of God as being the bedrock and cornerstone of all Human Laws.

If mankind is often bewildered today, that there is so much crime in society despite the proliferation of finely-crafted laws, it is basically because Man is constantly violating the Laws of Life. We will never be able to live healthy and peaceably among ourselves, however much we try to enforce man-made laws, so long as we ignore and break the Laws of Life. There is a war going on in the system of each person, and this war is what is simply being translated and transposed to our day-to-day interpersonal relationships.

This publication therefore gives the reader a taste of what God has given to the author to reveal to humanity about the simplicity and yet all pervasiveness of the Laws of Life. It is to be hoped that this Revelation will save a perverse world that keeps spinning out new laws to bring about a perfect society while these laws themselves are compiled by imperfect lawmakers and enforced by a whole spectrum hopelessly overwhelmed and often officials who are dangerously uninformed regarding the Laws of Life. It is the sincere hope of the author that this series of teachings will lead mankind to the discovery of the truth. For now, it would appear that without the knowledge of the truth, all the experts on jurisprudence, like the author himself once did, fall into the category that the Apostle Paul described in one of his letters to Timothy.

2 Timothy 3:7 King James Version (KJV)
[7] Ever learning, and never able to come to the knowledge of the truth.

CONTENTS

Law 1: *The Law of the Spirit of Life and the Law of Sin & Death*   1
Law 2: *The Law of Faith*   6
Law 3: *The Law of Resistance & Non-Resistance*   10
Law 4: *The Law of Sowing and Reaping*   15
Law 5: *The Law of Prayer*   19
Law 6: *The Law of Seasons*   16
Law 7: *The Law of Accountability and Responsibility*   25
Law 8: *The Law of Forgiveness*   29
Law 9: *The Law of Health*   32
Law 10: *The Law of Exaltation & Abasement*   35
Law 11: *The Law of Words*   38
Law 12: *The Law of Notice and Warning*   41
Law 13: *The Law of Captivity, Deliverance, & Restoration*   45
Law 14: *The Law of Love*   48
Law 15: *The Law of Agreement*   51
Law 16: *The Law of Vengeance*   54
Law 17: *The Law of Reward*   57
Law 18: *Spiritual Law & Mosaic Law*   60
Law 19: *Spiritual Law & Spiritual Warfare*   67
Law 20: *Spiritual Law & Grace*   70
Law 21: *Spiritual Law & Angels*   73
Law 22: *The Law of the Gift*   76
Law 23: *The Law of Mercy*   79
Law 24: *The Law of Authority*   82
Law 25: *The Law of Escape*   85
Law 26: *The Law of Success*   88
Law 27: *The Law of Work*   90
Law 28: *The Law of Bearability*   93
Law 29: *The Law of Service*   96

CONTENTS

Law 30: *The Law of Reputation and Character*	99
Law 31: *The Law of Waste and Want*	103
Law 32: *The Law of Worship*	107
Law 33: *The Law of Forfeiture*	111
Law 34: *The Law of Imputation*	114
Law 35: *The Law of Brokenness*	117
Law 36: *The Law of Truth*	120
Law 37: *The Law of Direction*	122
Law 38: *The Law of Completion*	124
Law 39: *The Law of Patterns*	126
Law 40: *The Law of Suffering*	129
Law 41: *The Law of Foreseeability*	132
Law 42: *Spiritual Law and Principles*	136
Law 43: *Spiritual Law and the Prophetic*	139
Law 44: *The Law of Overstepping*	141
Law 45: *The Law of Provocation*	143
Law 46: *The Law of Delegability and Non-Delegability*	145
Law 47: *Law of Contamination*	148
Law 48: *Law of Corruption*	151
Law 49: *Law of Confirmation*	153
Law 50: *Law of Provision*	156
Fred's Testimony	162

LAW 1

The Law of the Spirit of Life and the Law of Sin and Death

Romans 8:2 (KJV)

For the law of the Spirit of Life in Christ Jesus hath made me free from the law of sin and death.

LAW OF THE SPIRIT OF LIFE AND THE LAW OF SIN AND DEATH

Everybody walking and breathing on the surface of the earth today, regardless of education, wealth, or any other consideration, is operating under one of two laws: "The Law of the Spirit of Life in Christ Jesus or the Law of Sin and Death". There is no in between. You are either under the Law of the Spirit of Life in Christ or the Law of Sin and Death. Initially, Adam and Eve were under the Law of the Spirit of Life until they disobeyed God which then put them under the Law of Sin and Death. But based upon what Jesus did for us on the cross, we are restored to the Law of the Spirit of Life in Christ Jesus.

There is only one way we can get out of The Law of Sin and Death and that is to invoke The Law of the Spirit of Life in Christ Jesus by accepting Jesus as our Savior and Lord. It does not matter if you were born into a Christian family, or how many family members you have who are Christians, you do not automatically qualify for acquittal under the Law of the Spirit of Life in Christ Jesus.

The Law of the Spirit of Life and the Law of Sin and Death are the most important of all laws in Creation. If one tries to live under any law other than the Law of the Spirit of Life, they will ultimately fail and they will be held accountable under the Law of Sin and Death.

A person does not have sufficient self-control or will to resist sin under their own power. There is nothing as humans that we can do on our own to withstand sin no matter how hard we try. Paul teaches us that all humanity has a corrupt nature incapable of perfect obedience to God's Will.

We need faith in Christ to be removed from the Law of Sin and Death. God became man to save us from sin (Matt.1:21) and that through faith in the atoning blood of Christ we receive forgiveness of sin. Human beings are not forgiven by their own merit but by the saving grace of God. The consequences of being under the Law of Sin and Death is eternal death, whereas being under the Laws of the Spirit of Life is eternal life.

That does not mean that we abuse the gift by sinning more.(Romans 6:1) It means the God's Spirit in us gives us the strength to resist sin. Though we can never completely live free from corruption, we can work toward a sinless life as our goal. (I John 1:3)

Examples:

<u>Lot and His Wife</u>

Lot and his family lived in Sodom. God planned to destroy Sodom because of the evil there. Lot was not a perfect man, but he had some redeeming qualities and if there had been even ten other righteous men in the city, the city would have been saved. They were not to be found, so the angels told Lot to take his family away from the city. The family ran away from Sodom. The angels warned everyone in the family to not look back. Lot's wife disobeyed. After they had gone from Sodom, Lot's wife stopped and looked back at the city. As a result, Lot's wife turned into a pillar of salt. She had the opportunity for life but she disobeyed God and looked back at her old life. Many are so tied to the old life, (sin and death) that they are unwilling to accept the new life that only comes from the Spirit of Life in Christ Jesus.

Paul, The Apostle

Paul, who after his conversion, became a predominant leader and builder of the Christian Church, began as a Jewish religious zealot. He was a persecutor of Christians. He would be considered a religious terrorist. He was trained in the Mosaic Law and was skilled in persuading people. On the way to Damascus, he met Jesus and lost his sight. As a blind man, others with him had to guide him. Jesus sent him to Ananias. Ananias was afraid to meet him because of Paul's reputation. God told Ananias that Paul would be greatly used by God and further Christianity. Ananias obeyed God and taught Paul. Because Paul had great skill in questioning and answering techniques, he was able to be very persuasive. Paul changed his life completely and dedicated his life to spreading the Gospel. Though Paul was under sin and death, it all changed when he met and accepted Jesus and His teachings. Through Jesus, he gained life.

Rich Man, Poor Man

A rich man and a poor man died. The rich man was in Hell and Lazarus the beggar was in Abraham's bosom. The rich man saw this and begged Abraham to let Lazarus come and dip his finger in water to cool his tongue.

Abraham told him that he had a lifetime of riches while Lazarus had nothing but evil so now Lazarus is in my bosom, and you are in torment. Besides, there is a gulf between us which cannot be crossed. Luke 16:19-26… The poor man was on the side of the Spirit of Life in Christ Jesus and the rich man was on the side of Sin and Death for eternity.

LAW 2
The Law of Faith
Romans 3:27

Where is boasting then? It is excluded. By what law? of works? Nay: but by the law of faith.

LAW OF FAITH

Unless we operate on the positive side of this law, it is impossible to draw from the power of God. Faith attaches itself to and pulls from the power of God. We can cry all we want, or worry, day in and day out, stay up all night, walk the floor, prance and pace, but none of that will draw one iota from the power of God. We can discuss the situation or the circumstance with every family member or friend that we may have, that will not draw from the power of God. God has established a Law of Faith, and God has said to us, "If you want to draw from my power, I have established only one way for you to draw from that power, and that way is by operating through the Law of Faith."

Each person has enough faith in them to accept Christ. To have greater faith, one has to exercise and develop it. Unfortunately, most people operate on little faith. Because of this, people are missing out on many of the blessings God has to offer.

The basic principle of the Law of Faith is when you make a request from God, you have confirmation that it is in His Will, and it is consistent with His Word, that request is already answered in the spiritual realm, and we just have to be patient and receive it in God's perfect timing. We do not need to ask again. We just have to have faith.

Examples:

Woman with Issue of Blood

In Luke 8, we find the account of a woman who had an issue of blood for 12 years. She has spent all her resources on physicians and could not be healed by any. She came behind Jesus and touched the border of His garment and immediately her issue of blood stopped.

Jesus asked who touched me? When all around Him denied that they had, Peter said to Him, "Master, the multitude has pressed against you." Peter in essence was saying that it could have been one of many people. But Jesus said, "Somebody has touched me in **faith** because virtue has gone out of me."

This is a perfect example of how faith draws automatically from the power of God.

Faith of Noah and the Ark

(Genesis 6:14-22) God told Noah that the world was so corrupt that it was going to be destroyed with water and that he should build an ark with specifications that would house animals of every kind and his family. Noah did in faith exactly what God had instructed him to do. His family and the human race were spared.

The Interview

A Christian woman has an important interview for an employment opportunity. She is a single mother with small children. Her car will not start. She knows in her heart that God has promised her this job. She prays in faith that her vehicle will start, and she will make this important appointment on time. After several tries, the car finally starts, and she is on her way. Her faith pulled from the power of God and her car started.

On a Wing and a Prayer

In the movie "On a Wing and a Prayer", a man and his family are traveling to a funeral. He had at least one lesson in flying a plane but was not very successful and decided that flying a plane was not for him, so that was to be his last lesson. While on the flight to his brother's funeral, the pilot had a heart attack and died. The man, played by Dennis Quaid, had to fly and land the plane.

He prayed for God to guide him and give him the presence of mind to land the plane safely and save his family. God put the right people in the right place at the right time to bring his family to a safe landing.

The father and his wife flew the plane believing God was with them and would help him. They were able to keep a cool head as they followed the instructions of a seasoned pilot. His faith not only resulted in saving his family's life, but he earned his pilot's license and flew all over the country delivering Bibles.

LAW 3
The Law of Resistance & Non-Resistance
Matthew 5:38-41

[38] "You have heard that it was said, 'An eye for an eye and a tooth for a tooth.' [39] But I tell you not to resist an evil person. But whoever slaps you on your right cheek, turn the other to him also. [40] If anyone wants to sue you and take away your tunic, let him have your cloak also. [41] And whoever compels you to go one mile, go with him two.

THE LAW OF RESISTANCE & NON-RESISTANCE

Under this law, we as believers are permitted to resist only when we have to react to something that violates the Word of God. Otherwise, we are completely under the Law of Authority as it relates to those individuals who are over us. This law suggests to us that we have no right to resist unless that person is requiring us to do something that violates the Word of God. In other words, we are to live under the laws set by our government, unless the law of the government defies the Word of God.

Supreme Court Case

A recent court case came before the Supreme Court about whether the USPS could make an employee work on Sunday. The employee's faith honors the commandment, "You shall remember the Sabbath Day and keep it holy." In his view, he would be going against his religion to work on Sunday. The USPS fired him. He lost benefits that he had earned. He took his case to court. The Supreme Court eventually heard his case and agreed with the employee. According to the Law of Resistance and Non-resistance, the employee did the right thing. If the Supreme Court had not ruled in his favor, the best thing for him to do would be to quit the job and find a new one that does not require working on Sunday.

Driver's License Renewal

On the other end of this, let's say a person doesn't think it is fair to renew his driver's license every 4 years. The Word of God does address when driver's licenses should be renewed. If the person does not renew his license and gets caught without one, he will get a fine. He has no recourse. He must follow the law or face the consequences of the law because the secular law dealing with this matter is not in conflict with the Law of Resistance and Non-resistance.

There are other times when being under the Law of Resistance and Non-resistance is less clear such as how our taxes are used. A person may agree with paying their taxes but is the money used for purposes that are clearly against the Will of God. For these, there is much controversy. In the end, it is important to know and understand God's Word and if you do not agree with how the money is used, then you have the power of the vote. You can work to make your voice heard and lawfully work to keep spending in line with the values of the country. Your conscience would need to lead you. Not paying taxes would not be wise.

Examples:

Paul's Imprisonment

In Acts 16, a damsel possessed with the spirit of divination followed Paul and Silas for many days. Paul, being grieved, turned and said to the spirit, "I command you in the Name of Jesus Christ to come out of her and it came out. The damsel's masters became angry with Paul and Silas because of the money they were making as a result of the damsel's fortune telling.

The crowd brought Paul and Silas to the magistrates and were commanded to be beaten. They beat Paul and Silas and threw them into prison. After Paul and Silas prayed and sang, God brought an earthquake, the prison doors opened and Paul and Silas were released, and the keeper of the prison was saved.

The next day, the magistrate ordered Paul and Silas to be let go and to release them by way of the back door. Under the law of resistance and non-resistance, Paul being a Roman citizen and now a Christian having been unjustly beaten and condemned, openly resisted. He demanded that he be brought out by the way he was taken in, which was the front door, because he is now a kingdom representative.

Use of Lunchtime

An employee goes out into the yard on his lunch break to read the Bible and pray. The employer objects to him going out and reading the Bible and praying. The employee resists the warning and is willing to accept being fired if need be.

Obey God rather than man and be willing to accept man's consequences.

LAW 4
The Law of Sowing & Reaping
Galatians 6:7

Be not deceived; God is not mocked: for whatsoever a man soweth, that shall he also reap.

THE LAW OF SOWING AND REAPING

Whatever I do to you is what is going to come back to me. That is why the Word says, "Do unto others as you would have others do unto you." If what you are about to sow is not what you want as a consequence, nor what you want as a harvest, then you should not do it to another person.

Human beings can be fooled, so we are told not to be tricked. If you put your faith in the flesh or anything other than Christ, then you are depending on your own self will. Those who depend on Christ completely receive salvation and the blessings of God.

There is a positive and a negative side to the Law of Sowing and Reaping. The good things you do will come back to you in the same form you sowed your positive seed. The negative things you do will also be returned in a like manner. We also know that they will be in the same vein as the action was put out, but the action will also be multiplied. If you sow sparingly, your yield will be small. If you sow generously, in a way that will bless others, and you will be generously blessed. II Corinthians 9:6-7 That tells us that there is a positive and a negative side to the Law of Sowing and Reaping. Fortunately, because of God's mercy, a Christian will not necessarily receive what he/she may deserve.

Examples:

Instill Faith in Children

If you teach your children or talk to friends about your faith in God, you sow a seed in them that may eventually lead them to Christ.

Too Much Change

A person receives too much change. Her first response is to return it when she discovers the mistake. She gets busy and doesn't return it. The consequences are that she will also incur a loss and it will be greater than what she did not return.

Jacob and Laban

Jacob had become a trickster and a schemer and had conned his brother out of his birthright. The tables were turned on him by his father-in-law, Laban. Jacob bargained with Laban for Rachael to be his wife. Laban deceived him and caused Jacob to have to work for Rachael and Leah for fourteen years.

An Employer Who Takes Advantage

An employer takes advantage of his employees by paying them much less than they are worth because of their desperation to have a job. As a result of the employer's unfavorable reputation concerning his employees, a supplier charges him much more for supplies.

Farmland Used for Church

Another example is of Frederick and his wife, Adele, who lived on a lovely farm. Near them there were railroad tracks. When the trains came, tramps would come to their house and ask for food. They were always prepared and always fed the men. They never forgot their tithe as well. Eventually, the woman opened a Sunday School which evangelized many young people in the community. Many came to Christ. Years passed and the couple have been with their Father in Heaven for many years. Over the years, the farmland went through different hands. Today, a huge church has been built on the land. People come from all over to find the Lord. The couple's great grandson, Justin, became the associate pastor. Only God could know the fruits of the couple's prayers and faithfulness.

LAW 5

The Law of Prayer
1 John 5:14, 15

¹⁴ And this is the confidence that we have in him, that, if we ask any thing according to his will, he heareth us:
¹⁵ And if we know that he hear us, whatsoever we ask, we know that we have the petitions that we desired of him.

THE LAW OF PRAYER

Prayer is not supposed to be happenstance or coincidence. Most of us have scattergun prayers. We throw a bunch of prayers out there hoping that God hears one or more of them, and that we will get the desired result by and by. This is treating prayer like the fast food system. We want it quick, fast and in a hurry. We do not want to tarry. We do not want to wait to get a revelation as to what God's will is in that particular circumstance. The prayers that Jesus prayed were always answered because he prayed for the perfect Will of the Father.

When we pray, our faith should assure us that our prayer is answered. We do not need to insult God by asking for the same thing over and over. If we pray with a confirmation that what we are praying for is within the Will of God, our prayer is consistent with who God is and with His Word, we can be confident that our prayer is first answered in the spiritual realm and will be manifested in the physical world according to God's perfect timing.

Examples:

Hezekiah

Hezekiah was told by the prophet Isaiah that he was going to die. He immediately turned to the wall and began praying. He reminded God how he had served him and had expectations that his prayer would be answered. His prayer was answered and he was told that he had added 15 years to his life.

Prayers for Healing

Prayers from family members who pray for John to be healed from cancer are answered. He becomes healed and can return to a normal life.

Prayer of the Church

Acts 12 tells of when King Herod had arrested Peter to satisfy the Jews. The church began praying continuously. God heard them and sent an angel to rescue Peter. He was in prison bound in chains and between two soldiers. The angel took Peter and the soldiers did not realize he was gone until morning.

A Student Enters College

A young Christian college student was the first in his family to pursue higher education. He is very concerned that he will not be able to keep up because of his limited educational and social background. He prays without ceasing. His prayers are answered. At the end of his freshman year, he makes the honor roll and remains on the honor roll throughout his college years. He gives God the Glory.

LAW 6
The Law of Seasons
Ecclesiastes 3:1-8

1 To every thing there is a season, and a time to every purpose under the heaven: 2 A time to be born, and a time to die; a time to plant, and a time to pluck up that which is planted; 3 A time to kill, and a time to heal; a time to break down, and a time to build up; 4 A time to weep, and a time to laugh; a time to mourn, and a time to dance; 5 A time to cast away stones, and a time to gather stones together; a time to embrace, and a time to refrain from embracing; 6 A time to get, and a time to lose; a time to keep, and a time to cast away; 7 A time to rend, and a time to sew; a time to keep silence, and a time to speak; 8 A time to love, and a time to hate; a time of war, and a time of peace.

LAW OF SEASONS

We easily relate to certain things in nature concerning seasons. There are certain things we do in certain seasons. We understand, accept and adhere to natural seasons. But because we can not make contact with Spiritual seasons with our natural senses, most believers are unaware that these Spiritual Seasons are just as real as the natural seasons that we know and respect.

One can only know and understand these spiritual seasons, by being in tune with God's Spirit and acknowledging Christ as Source, accepting His sacrifice, and keeping faith in all that God is. He works through His Spirit in us to help us understand our seasons and to make the most of them. He guides us and helps us grow into the person He wants us to be, which is like He himself is. We can never reach perfection, but our goal is to be Christlike. We can only do this through the Spirit of God indwelling in us.

Many believers are operating out of the Law of Seasons and have not used an understanding of the seasons to lead a more full productive life. Once one understands the seasons then they must allow the Spirit of God to work in them and exercise their faith.

Examples:

<u>Times and Seasons</u>

God changes times and seasons; He removes kings and appoints kings; He gives wisdom and knowledge to the wise. Daniel 2:21

Close to God

Sometimes you feel so close to God. You feel like the sky's the limit in productivity. Sometimes you wonder where God is, why is He letting such terrible things happen to you, then You may feel you are gaining growth or just resting in Him. All these are God's seasons.

Moving to a New Home

John had a revelation that he was to move to a small town in Tennessee. Everytime he thought he was ready for the move something came up and prevented him. This went on for a number of years. The day finally came when he was able to get it all together and was able to make the move. Upon arrival in his new city, he found everything in place, an apartment, job, church family, and friends. He realized the reason for the delay was that God was putting things in order and it was not the season previously, but now it's the right time for him to move to Tennessee.

LAW 7
The Law of Accountability & Responsibility
Romans 14:12

So then every one of us shall give account of himself to God.

THE LAW OF ACCOUNTABILITY AND RESPONSIBILITY

Everything we say, everything we do, brings us under the Law of Accountability and Responsibility. Believers have to be mindful of daily activities, what we do, what we fail to do, or what we are involved in because we are accountable for what we do and what we fail to do. The Word tells us that we are accountable for every idle word we speak. Most believers do not want to acknowledge accountability in spiritual matters. Tragically, we fail to understand that there is an accountability and responsibility in the spirit realm and we are accountable to God for everything we do or say.

We can never shift the blame to another person. We may try in the material world, most of the time you will be found out. There is no use trying to pass the blame in the spiritual world because God sees, hears, and knows everything.

Fortunately for us, God judges our actions upon our own merit and our ability to do so. If we are given great intellect our accountability is greater as far as using it in our gift. If a person's intelligence is at a lower level, God meets you where you are. God's perfect wisdom assures fair judgement. This is true with all our gifts, we are judged at the level of our ability.

Examples:

Accountability for Sin

… every man shall be put to death for his own sin. Deuteronomy 24:16

Providing for Family

-If a person does not provide for his own household, he has denied the faith and is worse than an unbeliever. I Timothy 5:8

-Thomas became very ill. Over time, he became unable to work and support his family. It put a hardship on his family. His wife started to work to support the family. Thomas felt disheartened. He worked extremely hard to become well again. He knew taking care of his family was an important responsibility. A person's work gives a person his identity and self-respect. It wasn't easy, but he regained health and was able to return to work. He knew that working is respected in the community and was pleasing to God.

Truth

A man had an affair and asked a friend to lie for him. The friend refused because he knew he was accountable for his own actions. If he agreed to lie, then he would be in agreement with the friend's actions and be accountable for it.

Prayer Partners

Ralph and Jerry are prayer partners. They have agreed to pray together every morning and to make themselves accountable and responsible to each other, not only to pray, but to share matters of concern.

Job Responsibilities

Jim agreed to open the office every day at a certain time. He was not required to do so but volunteered. On this particular morning, Jim had not been feeling well and did not open the office, so it caused an inconvenience to all of the workers. Jim did not arrange for anyone else to open the office. He had an obligation to open or notify someone if he could not open the office. Based on the practice that Jim had initiated, can he be held accountable?

LAW 8

The Law of Forgiveness
Mark 11:26

But if ye do not forgive, neither will your Father which is in heaven forgive your trespasses.

THE LAW OF FORGIVENESS

Forgiveness is a gift God gives us freely and completely. We are also to forgive others freely and completely. Because He gives us grace for Christ's sake, we are to also give grace to others. In that way, we show our relationship to God. When we are forgiven by God, the sin is not remembered by Him anymore. Sins against us which are forgiven are not to be remembered. Unforgiveness breaks down our relationships and interferes with God's purpose for us.

Believers cannot afford unforgiveness. If you do not forgive those who offend you, then your prayers are hindered. We cannot expect God to answer our prayers, if we do not maintain our relationship with God. Unforgiveness is too costly. The Law of

Forgiveness is also referred to in the Sermon on the Mount. (Matthew 6:12) Our willingness to forgive shows our true relationship with Him. It makes our prayers more powerful.

If we as Christians are unforgiving, our ability to witness to others is damaged. We lose our credibility as a person who has been saved by Grace. We never earn our salvation or forgiveness. Unforgiveness has to do with relationship, faith, and credibility.

Examples:

Joseph and His Brothers

Joseph forgave his brothers for stealing his coat and selling him and later saved his family from starvation. Joseph was a man who gained favor with God. Genesis 50:15-21

Jesus on the Cross

As Jesus died on the cross, He asked that those that crucified Him be forgiven. Luke 23:34

Maria's Heavy Heart

Forgiveness is not always easy. Maria knew a woman who was cruel to someone in her family and caused him harm. Maria knew the woman had some emotional problems, but the harm she caused seemed neverending. It was important for Maria to forgive the woman because Maria's unforgiveness was negatively impacting Maria's testimony. Eventually, with the help of God and a very wise pastor, Maria was able to forgive the woman and the heaviness in Maria's heart was lifted.

Unforgiveness Prevented Healing

A woman suffered from a problem with her stomach. She told her pastor that her doctors could not find the cause. She had prayed for healing. Her friends and family also prayed for her. She talked to her pastor and he said that maybe there was someone who she had not forgiven and that was preventing her healing. She couldn't think of anyone that she hadn't forgiven. She searched her heart and remembered a person that had bullied her in school and it still layed on her heart and when she thought of it, she felt hurt. She took it to God, forgave that person and after a short while her stomach problem disappeared.

LAW 9

The Law of Health

Proverbs 4:20-22

My son, attend to my words; incline thine ear unto my sayings.
Let them not depart from thine eyes; keep them in the midst of thine heart.
For they are life unto those that find them, and health to all their flesh.

THE LAW OF HEALTH

The Foundational Scripture for the Law of Health is about King Solomon passing on words of wisdom to his son. He wants to make sure that his son realizes how important God's Word is. We should be in the Word daily, meditate on it and keep it close to our hearts.

The Word of God is life and health to all our flesh. The Spirit of God will reveal to us those things that we do in the natural, emotionally and spiritually, that either adhere to laws of health or violate laws of health.

Attending to our health in body, mind, and spirit is extremely important as one affects the others. If any part of who we are is not in balance, we are not able to be who we are meant to be. None of the 3 parts of who we are should be neglected.

Examples:

Honor God with Our Bodies
In Jeremiah, it says that we are to honor God with our bodies. We belong to God and our bodies belong to Him. He will heal us of our wounds.

Bodies are Temples

Our bodies are temples of the Holy Spirit. You are not your own. I Corinthians 6: 19-20

A Pastor Dealing With Stress

A pastor dealing with lots of stress doesn't watch his weight and gradually his weight grows to an unhealthy level. A member of his congregation gives him the book "Eating God's Way." He decides that his weight makes him less effective in his calling and hurts his testimony. Following God's plan he gets to a healthy balance.

An Athlete's Teeth

Calvin was a young strong athlete in several sports and was popular in his high school. Calvin had beautiful strong brilliant white teeth. Oftentimes, in an effort to impress, he would open soft drinks by using his teeth to lift the cap. Calvin continued to do this for many years. Because of this activity, there came a time when he lost his front teeth. His healthy looking teeth were destroyed because of his pride and violation of the Law of Health.

LAW 10

The Law of Exaltation & Abasement
Matthew 23:12

And whosoever shall exalt himself shall be abased; and he that shall humble himself shall be exalted.

THE LAW OF EXALTATION AND ABASEMENT

The Body of Christ, in many instances today, is functioning according to the world's system as it relates to Spiritual Law. Most of us are our own public relations persons. We are blowing our own trumpets and we are tooting our own horns, just as the world does. This is a great violation of The Law of Exaltation and Abasement. When we operate on the negative side of this law, we automatically bring ourselves under The Law of Abasement or being brought low.

The Law of Exaltation and Abasement is difficult to navigate in a day when social media and technology makes it easy for us to put ourselves in front of people with all our achievements and exciting things we do. It is difficult not to brag about ourselves. It is almost expected that you will exalt yourself on social media and if you are trying to sell something you want to build your brand. People buy you more than they buy the product.

At what point does sharing information about yourself cross the line? It crosses the line when you exalt yourself above others and above God. One has to keep a check on your own heart to know when the line is crossed. The result of exalting yourself above God leads to abasement. You will receive negative results from exalting yourself. When you put yourself above others, most likely someone will bring you down. You may get overlooked. People may think you are lying. A person may lose friends because a braggart is not pleasant to be around.

Examples:

<u>Job Remains Humble</u>

Job 40:11-12 "Pour out the overflowing of your anger, and look on everyone who is proud and make him low." Rich or poor, bad health or good health, Job remained humble and faithful to God.

For everyone who exalts himself will be humbled, and he who humbles himself will be exalted. Luke 14:11

Mark Loses Contract

Mark boasts about all the things he has accomplished in his life. Others begin to doubt him; they even think maybe he is not telling the truth. When he applies for a new contract, he is not chosen because of his pride.

Shirley's Voice

Shirley had a beautiful voice and was one of the lead singers in her church choir. She was proud of the accolades she received and was the lead singer on every song. The choir was having its annual concert and Shirley was very excited at her opportunity to show off before her family and friends. She was overly confident and as Shirley led the first song, she forgot the words, was embarrassed and had difficulty during the remainder of the concert. She was a dismal failure.

LAW 11
The Law of Words
Proverbs 18:21

Death and life are in the power of the tongue: and they that love it shall eat the fruit thereof.

THE LAW OF WORDS

Death and Life are in the power of the tongue. This implies that in everything we say we are speaking either life or death to that situation. Most believers are speaking death to daily circumstances. By our words, we are justified, and by our words, we are condemned.

Our words can cause happiness or sorrow. They can give hope or destroy hope. Unkind words said to a spouse or child can be devastating to the person or the opposite, kind words can lift a person. There are consequences to our words. A witness in court can cause a man to be condemned or be set free. A teacher can cause false beliefs or can put students on the right path. Undue criticism can cause others to doubt themselves.

We talk about death and life words in today's terms of being negative and positive words. Positive words encourage and lift up others, while negative words tear down and destroy.

Examples:

Words Used as Deception

The words of his mouth were smoother than butter, but war was in his heart, his words were softer than oil, yet were drawn swords. Psalms 55:21

Words Used Against Someone

In Luke 20:20, they were watching Jesus's words so they could have justification to deliver Jesus to the Governor.

Discouragement

June, Jason's mom, gets frustrated easily especially when she is drinking and tells Jason he cannot do anything right. Jason feels he can never accomplish anything. He does poorly in school and drops out before he graduates.

Words Cannot Be Taken Back

Janie was in a bad mood. She said some hurtful things to Maria who had frequently helped her. Maria was deeply hurt by the words Janie said. Later, Janie regretted it. Maybe Janie should have apologized but chose to forget what she said to Maria. Even an apology probably wouldn't have taken away the pain of what Janie said to Maria. Words hurt and once spoken, they cannot be undone.

Carrie's Critical Spirit

Carrie has a critical spirit and constantly thinks and speaks negative words about herself, people around her, and events. She has been told by her friends that she is framing her world by negativity. Carrie can not understand why her life seems to go from bad to worse.

LAW 12

The Law of Notice & Warning

Amos 3:7

Surely the LORD God will do nothing, but he revealeth his secret unto his servants the prophets.

THE LAW OF NOTICE AND WARNING

God said, I will not do anything unless I first reveal it to my servants, the prophets. God is saying to us that anything that He does which is not reserved to Himself, He will reveal to one of His. Under the Law of Notice and Warning, Our God, Our Heavenly Father, has committed Himself to not allow His children to be caught by surprise.

He gives us notice and warning through natural means such as clouds letting us know what kind of weather to expect or the changing of the color of leaves indicating the coming of fall. He also uses man made inventions or signs in our environment. A sign on a mountain road saying 'falling rocks' puts one on the look out for danger ahead. He will use other people to advise us, dreams, angels, and even a small voice in our spirit. These are just a few ways he gives us notice and warning.

The Law of Notice and Warning operates on a positive and a negative side. While notice gives us something to look forward to, a warning lets us know to be careful when something concerning is on its way.

We can learn to listen to God's warnings or we can choose not to. As we grow as Christians, we become more sensitive to notice and warning and are better able to discern the notice and warning that come from God. If you look or even think back at circumstances, you can remember times when if you had just listened to that little voice inside, you would have avoided an unpleasant or harmful situation.

Examples:

Lot and his family were told that when he and his family left the city that they were not to look back. Lot's wife looked back and was turned into a pillar of salt. They ignored the warning. Genesis 19

The Cock's Crow

Peter was told by Jesus, *"I tell you, Peter, the cock will not crow this day, until you three times deny you know me."* LUKE 22:34 When men asked Peter if he was a disciple of Christ. He said, "I do not know the man." After the third time, the cock crowed. Peter "wept bitterly" but he had been warned. Matthew 26:75

Jeremy's Inner Voice

Jeremy had a bad feeling when he got into his car. He knew a storm was coming, but he thought that he could go ahead and make it back home before it started. Before it began to snow, it began raining. He saw the rain but wanted to finish his shopping before he headed home. What he didn't know was that the temperature was dropping and the rain was turning to ice. He got in his car and started home. It was slow going. Before he got home, he slid off the highway and wrecked his car.

Street Sign

A sign says to drive 25 mph in a residential zone but Matt drives 40 mph. There are cars parked on both sides of the street. A child runs into the street and is hit by the car. The driver had warning.

Steven's Dream

Steven was called to preach the gospel. He had a dream that he was standing before large crowds in different locations around the world. He had had this dream on several occasions. The reality was that he only had a Tuesday night Bible study with less than 10 people in attendance. Years later, as his ministry expanded he looked over a crowd of thousands. He remembered the notice he had received and that it had come to pass.

LAW 13

The Law of Captivity, Deliverance, & Restoration

2 Chronicles 7:14

¹⁴If my people, which are called by my name, shall humble themselves, and pray, and seek my face, and turn from their wicked ways; then will I hear from heaven, and will forgive their sin, and will heal their land.

THE LAW OF CAPTIVITY, DELIVERANCE & RESTORATION

Sin will automatically result in some form of bondage or captivity. The only way to reverse captivity is to confess, repent, rely on mercy, and make restitution where possible. Another component of deliverance is restoration, which completes the process of returning a person to his former place or condition.

We are to pray in humility to be free from sin, seek God's face and turn from sin which indicates true repentance. Only by turning from sin as proof of true repentance will one receive restoration. This applies to an individual as well as to a nation.

Examples:

A Nation in Captivity

Without exception, the children of Israel got into sin. God raised up a nation to bring them into captivity. When they confessed and repented, God would always deliver them from the hands of their captors. Not only would they be delivered, but God would always restore them with more than they had prior to being taken into boundage. It is the same with us today.

King David's Adultery

King David, a man after God's own heart, committed adultery with the wife of Uriah, had him killed and stole his wife. He was told by the prophet that the sword would never leave his house. King David then began to experience the negative harvest of his actions. As a result of his repentance he was delivered and even restored to his kingship, although he still continued to pay a price for his offense. II Samuel 11

Stolen Money for a Gambling Debt

Barbara was treasurer for a community drama club which she loved. She thought she could borrow a little of the money to cover a gambling debt. As time went on, she borrowed money over and over thinking that she would soon hit a big one at the casino and be able to repay it. At the end of the year, an accountant checked the books and Barbara was exposed. She was convicted of the crime and went to prison. While in prison, she became a Christian and was determined to make up for what she had done. Not long after her release, Barbara found employment. Over a period of time she was able to repay her debt to the drama club. She also received forgiveness from the club members. She was greatly appreciative of being forgiven.

Law 14
The Law of Love
1 Corinthians 13:8

Charity never faileth: but whether there be prophecies, they shall fail; whether there be tongues, they shall cease; whether there be knowledge, it shall vanish away?

THE LAW OF LOVE

Love never fails. It is an absolute. At no time, under any circumstances, regardless of what the situation may be, love never fails.

In the Bible, we read about three kinds of love: the love God has for human beings, human love for God, and love between humans. We also know that 'God is Love' (I John 4:8). Because He is love, love is in every aspect of God in who He is and what He does. His love is boundless. The greatest manifestation of His love is in the sacrifice of His Son, Jesus through whom we can have eternal life. Man's love for God is expressed through gratitude, worship, and obedience to His Word. Human beings love each other through acceptance and by serving and caring for each other.

Sometimes charity or love will feel cold because of our sin, but love is always there. A person may not nourish and take care of love because they let the things of this world take a more important role. Regardless, love is ever present. Love cannot be destroyed. Love lives through all of our temptations and our most difficult times. Love is forever perfect.

Examples:

God's Unfailing Love

Job knew God's love was unfailing. Even though everything was taken from him, Job maintained his obedience and faithfulness. Eventually, everything was restored to him and his blessings were multiplied. Book of Job

God gave His only son to die that we can live forever with Him. What greater love than that? John 3:16

A Life Changed

Bob, Mazie's son, has had a lot of trouble in school. He dropped out and began selling drugs. Mazie continued to pray for her son. Nevertheless, he was arrested and went to prison. Mazie never stopped seeing him and never stopped praying. Ten years later, Bob returned home. He had changed his life. Mazie never let her love fall from him.

Love Keeps Others From Sin

If a man was asked to lie for a friend, lying for him would not be showing love because love doesn't come from sin.

Love Can Be Restored

Lizzie is a widow with several children. Her oldest daughter was very rebellious and angry with God because of her father's untimely death. This daughter was very disrespectful to her mother, talked down to her, stole from her, and would be missing for days. Through it all, Lizzie continued to extend unlimited love to this daughter. Years passed and because of love and prayer, this daughter began to change. She became a Christian and she and Lizzie now have a loving mother daughter relationship.

LAW 15

The Law of Agreement
Amos 3:3

Can two walk together, except they be agreed?

THE LAW OF AGREEMENT

In life, I "walk" with everything, whether by affiliation or association. I have set myself in agreement with everything I am involved in, which includes educational, religious and political activities. In worldly parlance, birds of a feather flock together. So in everything I commit myself to, either knowingly or unknowingly, I bring myself under The Law of Agreement and I am therefore accountable for my actions.

If we walk with another person, we assume that there is a relationship with that person. We may have made common arrangements or be headed in the same direction. The relationship implies commonality between the two. The same is with God. He expects that if we walk with Him, we also have a relationship with Him. Whether in an activity or with another person or with God, if two walk together it shows agreement and relationship.

Examples:

Blessed is the man who walks not in the counsel of the ungodly. Psalm 1:1

Again I say unto you that if two of you shall agree on earth as touching any thing that they shall ask, it shall be done for them by my Father which is heaven. Matthew 18:19

In Business Together is an Agreement

Two men start a business. Their idea on how the business should be run is vastly different. One is inclined to cheat customers and the other perceives that as stealing. After a short time, the business fails.

Over Charge

A woman needs her battery replaced quickly, because she has to get to an important meeting. The mechanic replaces her battery but also does more repairs to which she did not agree. The mechanic and the customer were not in agreement or walking together.

Judgement of the Faith of Another

Mary has some mobility issues and has difficulty walking. She has been praying and exercising her faith for healing of her ankles and knees. She decided to apply for and received a handicapped sticker for her automobile. Some members of her Christian faith group disagreed with her using this handicapped sticker. They say to her that she has come into agreement with her disability by accepting and displaying the handicapped sticker. What do you say to this?

LAW 16

The Law of Vengeance

Romans 12:19

Dearly beloved, avenge not yourselves, but rather give place unto wrath: for it is written, Vengeance is mine; I will repay, saith the LORD.

THE LAW OF VENGEANCE

The Word of God says "vengeance is mine, saith the Lord". This implies that if we take vengeance ourselves, we have not only violated a sacred law, but taken what belongs to God, thereby possibly incurring His wrath. We as believers are to let God do the repaying and not us.

God can see in a man's heart so He knows all the circumstances around what a person does. He can see the whole picture where we as humans cannot. His judgement is perfect. Since God is also love, He is capable of greater mercy if it is warranted.

Examples:

King Saul and David

In I Samuel 24, we find that King Saul, because of his mental instability and jealousy towards David, hunted him on many occasions and tried to kill David. David had an opportunity to take revenge on Saul, but he did not. Instead, he said to Saul *"Now my father, see! Indeed, see the edge of your robe in my hand! For in that I cut off the edge of your robe and did not kill you, know and perceive that there is no evil or rebellion in my hands, and I have not sinned against you, though you are lying in wait for my life to take it. May the Lord judge you and me, and may the Lord avenge me on you; but my hand shall not be against you. As the proverb of the ancient says, 'Out of wicked comes forth wickedness' but my hand shall not be against you."* I Samuel 24:11-16 David although he would have been justified to do so, would not take revenge on God's anointed.

Never pay back evil for evil to anyone. Respect what is right in the sight of men. If possible, so far as it depends on you, be at peace with all men. *Never take your own revenge, beloved, but leave room for the wrath of God, for it is written. "Vengeance is mine, I will repay," says the Lord.* Hebrews 10:30

Hit and Run Accident

Brent's son was in an accident. A hit and run driver hit him while he was riding his bike home from school. His son survived, but is confined to a wheelchair with no hope of recovery. Brent spent most of his time obsessing over finding the driver. He followed any and every clue. His hatred and need for revenge made him neglect his son and his wife. His family needed him for his love and support but he seemed to have no love or time to spend with them. Ultimately, his wife divorced him and he no longer had a close relationship with his son. He lost everything because of his obsession and his need to get revenge.

Feeling Cheated

John felt cheated by a friend who he felt overcharged him for a lawn mower that only worked a short while. He resented the friend and no longer called him and had an attitude that was vengeful. The vengeance that John held in his heart will ultimately result in a negative consequence.

LAW 17
The Law of Reward
Matthew 6:1

Take heed that ye do not your alms before men, to be seen of them: otherwise ye have no reward of your Father which is in heaven.

THE LAW OF REWARD

If you're giving to others for the expressed purpose of being seen by man, The Law of Reward says that you have absolutely no reward coming from your Father which is in Heaven. You will not receive a reward on earth or in heaven. Likewise, anything that we're doing for self-recognition violates The Law of Reward. Therefore we forfeit whatever reward we would have coming based upon our actions.

When we give or do good deeds that no one sees and that is done without recognition, according to the Law of Reward, you will be rewarded in heaven and on earth.

Examples:

Behold, the Lord God will come with might, with His arm ruling for Him. Behold, His reward is with Him and His recompense be with Him. Isaiah 40:10

Blessed are you when people insult you, persecute you and falsely say all kinds of evil against you because of me. Rejoice and be glad, because great is your reward in heaven. Matthew 5:11-12

Linda's Attention for Good Deeds

Linda does lots of wonderful things for people. She gives generously to her church, buys toys for children whose names she draws from the Angel tree, takes food to the homeless, just to mention a few. With all the things she does, she also seeks attention for her good works. She always makes sure everyone knows what she is doing. She gets praise and admiration from everyone. Linda can choose to bring attention to herself and it makes her feel happy. Unaware of the Law of Reward, Linda believes she is laying a good foundation for rewards in heaven with all her kind deeds, however, her reward is of this earth. She has nothing coming from Father God. The Law of Reward clearly lays out that you do not receive your reward from God if you seek attention for your good deeds. Do your deeds in secret and do not make a big deal of them before others.

Tithing

Ross and Karen are the largest tithers in their assembly. They are faithful and generous in their obligation to tithe. Each Sunday, there is a section in the church bulletin listing tithers and the amount given. It gives Ross and his wife great pride to see their names on top of the list each Sunday. Have they received their reward?

We know that the church needs funds and people enjoy recognition, but in this case as many churches do by acknowledging tithing, are they encouraging Ross and Karen to lose their reward? To keep from the temptation of being puffed up about their tithing, they should ask the church to remove them from the list. If they ask to not be acknowledged and people find out and are recognized for it, in that case, because they were not seeking the reward they would not lose their reward from God. Every effort on their part should be done to keep their gift private.

Law 18
Spiritual Law & Mosaic Law
Exodus 20
The Ten Commandments

3 You shall have no other gods before me.

4 You shall not make for yourself an image in the form of anything in heaven above or on the earth beneath or in the waters below. 5 You shall not bow down to them or worship them; for I, the Lord your God, am a jealous God, punishing the children for the sin of the parents to the third and fourth generation of those who hate me, 6 but showing love to a thousand generations of those who love me and keep my commandments.

7 You shall not misuse the name of the Lord your God, for the Lord will not hold anyone guiltless who misuses his name.

8 Remember the Sabbath day by keeping it holy. 9 Six days you shall labor and do all your work, 10 but the seventh day is a sabbath to the Lord your God. On it you shall not do any work, neither you, nor your son or daughter, nor your male or female servant, nor your animals, nor any foreigner residing in your towns. 11 For in six days the Lord made the heavens and the earth, the sea, and all that is in them, but he rested on the seventh day. Therefore the Lord blessed the Sabbath day and made it holy.

12 Honor your father and your mother, so that you may live long in the land the Lord your God is giving you.

13 You shall not murder.

14 You shall not commit adultery.

15 You shall not steal.

16 You shall not give false testimony against your neighbor.

17 You shall not covet your neighbor's house. You shall not covet your neighbor's wife, or his male or female servant, his ox or donkey, or anything that belongs to your neighbor."

THE LAWS OF LIFE AND THE MOSAIC

All of the Mosaic (Laws of Moses) can be traced back to one or more Laws of Life which were established in the Garden of Eden. Mankind was under The Law of The Spirit of Life in the garden. When man fell, it brought him under the Law of Sin and Death. What Jesus did for us, by His death, burial and resurrection, returned us to The Law of The Spirit of Life in Christ Jesus and God's laws are now written on our hearts.

Jesus, being man and God, took all the sins of man on Himself. He took all the sins from the past, present, and future. He bore them and felt the guilt and pain of them. When that was accomplished, the return of the Spirit of Life was reestablished.

When Jesus was crucified, the veil was torn in the temple. Before that time, people had to make animal sacrifices to cover their sin so God could be with them. When Jesus was crucified, the price of man's sin was forever paid so God could be with man.

Jesus fulfilled the Mosaic law. He instructed us to love our neighbors as ourselves and to do unto others as you would have them do unto you. He said the greatest commandment was love.

Examples:

In the Sermon on the Mount, Jesus said, *You have heard it said ...referring to the Mosaic, but I say unto you... referring to spiritual law differentiating from the Mosaic law.* Matthew 5:7

Mosaic Law Used for Instruction

Jesus makes clear that the Mosaic was merely a school master written on tables of stone until the originally intended laws (carrying the Laws of Life) could be written on our hearts. All of the Ten Commandments merge into one law and that is the Law of Love. I Corinthians 13:13 *So faith, hope, love abide, these three; but the greatest of these is love.*

The Mosaic Laws merge with the Spiritual Laws of Life. Looking at the Ten Commandments, we can see how the commandments are also a part of the Spiritual Law. Let us look at each one and identify the spiritual Laws that go with them.

The Ten Commandments NKJV summarized followed by the related Spiritual Laws of Life.

1. You shall have no other gods before Me.
    - The Law of Love
    -The Law of Worship
    -The Law of Sowing and Reaping
    -The Law of Authority
    -The Law of Success
    -The Law of Spirit of Life

2. You shall not make gods or worship them.
    -The Law of Worship
    -The Law of Sowing and Reaping
    -The Law of Love
    -The Law of Success
    -The Law of Spirit of Life

3. You shall not use the Lord's name in vain.
    -The Law of Words
    -The Law of Love
    -The Law of Worship
    -The Law of Sowing and Reaping

-The Law of Success
-The Law of Spirit of Life

4. You shall keep the Sabbath Day holy.
   -The Law of Love
   -The Law of Worship
   -The Law Of Accountability and Responsibility
   -The Law of Sowing and Reaping
   -The Law of Health
   -The Law of Success
   -The Law of Spirit of Life

5. You shall honor your father and mother.
   -The Law of Love
   -The Law of Accountability and Responsibility
   -The Law of Sowing and Reaping
   -The Law of Authority
   -The Law of Success
   -The Law of Spirit of Life

6. You shall not murder.
   -The Law of Love
   -The Law of Accountability and Responsibility
   -The Law of Vengeance
   -The Law of Sowing and Reaping

-The Law of Reputation and Character
   -The Law of Success
   -The Law of Spirit of Life
7. You shall not commit adultery.
   -The Law of Love
   -The Law of Accountability and Responsibility
   -The Law of Sowing and Reaping
   -The Law of Agreement
   -The Law of Reputation and Character
   -The Law of Corruption
   -The Law of Contamination
   -The Law of Success
   -The Law of Spirit of Life

8. You shall not steal.
   -The Law of Love
   -The Law of Accountability and Responsibility
   -The Law of Sowing and Reaping
   -The Law of Reputation and Character
   -The Law of Corruption
   -The Law of Contamination
   -The Law of Success
   -The Law of Spirit of Life

9. You shall not give false witness against your neighbor.

-The Law of Love
-The Law of Accountability and Responsibility
-The Law of Words
-The Law of Sowing and Reaping
-The Law of Reputation and Character
-The Law of Corruption
-The Law of Contamination
-The Law of Success
-The Law of Spirit of Life

10. You shall not covet your neighbor's property.
    -The Law of Love
    -The Law of Accountability and Responsibility
    -The Law of Sowing and Reaping
    -The Law of Success
    -The Law of Spirit of Life

LAW 19

Spiritual Law & Spiritual Warfare
2 Corinthians 10:4

For the weapons of our warfare are not carnal, but mighty through God to the pulling down of strongholds.

THE LAWS OF LIFE AND SPIRITUAL WARFARE

The Word of God tells us that the weapons of our warfare are not carnal, meaning man made, but mighty through God to the pulling down of strongholds. We cannot fight or overcome the enemy by carnal weapons of the flesh, but only by and through spiritual weapons (which includes but are not limited to the full armour of God: prayer, binding and loosing, fasting, declaring, proclaiming and decreeing The Word of God).

Examples:

Jesus in the Wilderness

Jesus was under spiritual warfare when He was fasting in the wilderness for forty days and forty nights with no food and no water. Satan tempted Him by telling Him, Jesus could save Himself by asking the angels to minister to Him which was contrary to God's Will.

Warning of Spiritual Warfare

Alice knows she is going to face Spiritual Warfare everytime an occult type group comes to the door. She puts on the armor of God. Warfare takes the form of doubt, sickness, a family member having difficulties, etc. She puts on the armor of God through prayer and asks others to pray for her too.

A Nation's Plight

The United States and the entire world appear to be going through a time of spiritual warfare. Events are occurring that we know are not consistent and are against God's Laws. Yet people, even those believed to be good people, support the wrong path. It makes you wonder how they could possibly think the way they do and be so deceived.

Ephesians 6:12 *We wrestle not against flesh and blood, but against principalities, against powers, against rulers of darkness of this world, against spiritual wickedness in high places.*

II Corinthians 10:4 *The weapons of our warfare are not carnal but mighty through God to the pulling down of strongholds.*

Struggle with Suicide

Mary's son has been struggling with suicidal thoughts. These thoughts have been plaguing him for quite some time. His parents have been taking him for professional help from psychiatrists and psychologists but he has not improved. They finally realized that their son was under attack by a suicidal spirit. They finally took authority over the spirit by using the Word of God and now see results.

LAW 20
Spiritual Law & Grace
Ephesians 2:8-9

For by grace are ye saved through faith; and that not of yourselves: it is the gift of God:
Not of works, lest any man should boast.

SPIRITUAL LAW AND GRACE

Grace is considered to be a Divine favor we receive but do not deserve. Grace, however, comes under a Law of Life which is The Law of the Spirit of Life in Christ Jesus. The Gospel of Christ's birth and sacrifice is built upon God's grace. We cannot be saved without God's grace.

Though God is always gracious, the Old Testament deals with the Mosaic Law more than grace and the New Testament emphasizes grace more. John 1:17 *For the law was given through Moses; grace and truth came through Jesus Christ.*

Examples:

Changed Life

Saul persecuted Christians, but God came to him and he was saved by grace and his life was transformed.

Noah

In the time of Noah, people became so evil that God regretted creating man. God, however, knew Noah, a man of faith. God showed grace to Noah and he and his family were saved. The human race continued because of God's grace to Noah. Genesis 6

Lazarus

Lazarus was the brother of Martha and Mary, who Jesus often visited. While Jesus had been away for a while, Lazarus became ill and died; he was in the tomb for 4 days, however, Jesus raised him from the dead. Lazarus did nothing himself to be raised from the dead. He was returned to life by God's grace. *...by grace you have been saved.* Ephesians 2:5

Late Anointing

A woman in her seventies, who retired from teaching found a new career and was still able to work, earn, and make an impact to help others. She found her anointing late in life. This happened through grace, God's undeserved Divine favor.

LAW 21
Spiritual Law & Angels
Hebrews 1:14

Are they not all ministering spirits, sent forth to minister for them who shall be heirs of salvation?

THE LAWS OF LIFE AND ANGELS

Angels of God are spiritual beings who minister to the heirs of salvation. The only way they can be energized to function on our behalf is by us professing the Word of God to cause them to be activated in the circumstances of our lives.

Angels have three main roles. The first is to act as messengers. A few ways they communicate with people are in dreams, through other people and by appearing physically. They also take care of us by watching over us and protecting us. When you exercise your faith, angels will strengthen and comfort you. A third role that angels have is to record what we do and that may be presented on the Day of Judgement.

Examples:

Angels Give Warning to Lot

An angel told Abraham that Sodom and Gomorrah would be destroyed. Abraham negotiated with the Angel to save the cities if they could find 10 righteous people. The angels could not and they told Lot and his family to leave before the city was destroyed. Genesis 18

Angel Communicated with Paul

Peter was in prison and an angel came and removed his chains. The angel told him to get dressed, put on his sandals, wrap a cloak around himself, and follow him out of the prison. Acts 12:7

A Woman Comforted

Anna was terribly lonely. She was divorced and her children were visiting with their father. Anna had also moved so she could have a higher paying job. Her loneliness seemed more than she could bear. Anna prayed and prayed. An angel came and held her until she fell asleep. She never felt lonely in her life again.

Edward Received a Warning

Edward was driving through a shopping center parking lot and did not realize that he had come to the end of the shopping center lot and was about to enter a main street. He failed to see the stop sign as he entered this main thoroughfare. A speeding vehicle was within arm's reach of crashing into him. Suddenly, the oncoming driver was able to swerve and barely missed Edward's vehicle. He knew without a doubt that it was angelic protection that prevented what could have been a deadly accident.

LAW 22

The Law of the Gift
Proverbs 18:16

16 A man's gift maketh room for him, and bringeth him before great men.

LAW OF THE GIFT

God has given each of his children talents, special abilities and Spiritual gifts. There are primary gifts and there are secondary gifts. The secondary gifts are support gifts. Most believers operate outside of the gifts that God has given them. Our failures, professionally and otherwise, are as a result of our trying to operate in an area in which God has not called us.

We are given gifts and we choose to develop them or not. Our gifts add to life, give us enjoyment and make us happy. When God puts his anointing on our gift, then we can use it to bring people to Christ.

Examples:

Solomon's Primary Gift

King Solomon's primary gift per his request was the gift of wisdom. Solomon prayed for God to give him an understanding mind and to be able to discern between good and evil. His most well-known display of wisdom was when two women each claimed to be the mother of a baby. Solomon decided which mother was the actual mother by watching the woman react to his idea of cutting the baby in half and each one could have a half. The real mother did not want this to happen and gave her part up.
Solomon's secondary gift may have been the gift of administration. He was a great leader and he led his people not only in wisdom but with great success.

Paul's Gifts

Paul's primary gift was evangelism. His secondary gift was the gift of eloquence.

The Gift of Hospitality

Doris and Fred met when Doris accompanied Fred's singing by playing the organ for him in church. Both had individual gifts. Together they shared their gift of music and shared it with others. However, their primary gift was hospitality. There was no one who wasn't blessed by a visit to their home. Music supported their gift of hospitality.

<u>Prayer to Understand Anointing</u>

Shelby has many gifts. She can cook anything. She writes and speaks well. She is also an amazing artist. It would be difficult to list all her gifts. As a Christian, she is praying for God to show the anointing on the gift that would best serve God. When she receives confirmation of her anointing, she knows God will use her in miraculous ways.

LAW 23
The Law of Mercy
James 2:13

For he shall have judgment without mercy, that hath shewed no mercy; and mercy rejoiceth against judgment.

LAW OF MERCY

Mercy means that you do not get the judgment you deserve. We are going to reap what we sow, but God's mercy will allow us to reap at a lesser degree.

God is a God of judgement, and God knowing all things recognizes in His infinite wisdom that we are going to need mercy. This is what He has done; He allows, under Spiritual Law, for mercy to be a higher law than the law of judgement. You do not have to get what you deserve, because you can plead mercy, a move that can cause you to receive less of a consequence than you deserve.

Examples:

Israel's Complaint

The people of Israel in their exodus from Egypt complained because they did not have enough to eat. God in His mercy sent them manna which sustained them and filled their bellies. Exodus 16

Atonement for Sin

"For God so loved the world that He gave His only Son" with that He showed all men mercy. John 3:16

John Newton's Song

"Amazing Grace" was written by John Newton. He had been a slave trader, rapist, murderer. God saved John Newton by grace. He changed his life and became a man used by God. "Amazing Grace" remains today as one of the most sung hymns.

A Lighter Sentence

Alexander for years had been a recreational drug user. He was approached by one of his suppliers about being involved in selling to help pay for his drug use. Alexander thought about it for a while and decided why not? He participated in small drug sales for a while and graduated to larger volumes. He appeared to be successful. Later, he was set up by an undercover sting, arrested, and convicted. While awaiting sentencing, he gave his life to Christ, repented of his sins, and pleaded for mercy. His prayer was heard and he received a much lighter sentence than he could have received.

Law 24
The Law of Authority
Romans 13

1 Let every soul be subject unto the higher powers. For there is no power but of God: the powers that be are ordained of God.
2 Whosoever therefore resisteth the power, resisteth the ordinance of God: and they that resist shall receive to themselves damnation.
3 For rulers are not a terror to good works, but to the evil. Wilt thou then not be afraid of the power? do that which is good, and thou shalt have praise of the same:
4 For he is the minister of God to thee for good. But if thou do that which is evil, be afraid; for he beareth not the sword in vain: for he is the minister of God, a revenger to execute wrath upon him that doeth evil.
5 Wherefore ye must needs be subject, not only for wrath, but also for conscience sake.
6 For this cause pay ye tribute also: for they are God's ministers, attending continually upon this very thing.
7 Render therefore to all their dues: tribute to whom tribute is due; custom to whom custom; fear to whom fear; honour to whom honour.

THE LAW OF AUTHORITY

Believers are commanded to be subject unto 'The Higher Power' and that the powers that be are of God. When we resist the powers ordained of God (in government, the home, employment, the church, etc.)

we therefore are resisting God and are held accountable under the Law of Accountability and Responsibility.

We are to be good citizens and must submit to governing authorities. All authority comes from God and people in the positions of authority are placed there by God. Anyone not submitting to the authority that is anointed by God will receive a negative consequence. Those who are considered to be in their position by God's authority are those who are obedient to God.

There are three God-ordained authorities. They are in the home, the government, and the church. Each has a Divine purpose and problems occur when the leaders do not follow the purpose that God has for these institutions.

Examples:

<u>Noah's Obedience</u>

The people of Noah's time would not turn from idolatry and their wicked ways. Noah obeyed God by building a boat according to God's specifications even though people ridiculed him. Noah and his family survived. The rest of the world was destroyed in the flood.

Jesus Authority Revealed

Jesus gave us the Beatitudes in the Sermon on the Mount. He told us that He came to fulfill the law. Jesus showed His authority by the miracles He performed and His resistance to temptation.

David's Obedience

King David submitted himself to authority on the occasions that he had an opportunity to kill King Saul.

Lack of Respect for Authority in the Church

Dan was in a leadership position in his church. He had been in this position for several years and had seen pastors come and go. Dan often took issue with the pastors and often orchestrated against their agenda. As years passed, his children, now teenagers, began to rebel against him. He did not see the relationship between him resisting the authority of the pastors and his children rebelling against him.

LAW 25

The Law of Escape
1 Corinthians 10:13

13 There hath no temptation taken you but such as is common to man: but God is faithful, who will not suffer you to be tempted above that ye are able; but will with the temptation also make a way to escape, that ye may be able to bear it.

LAW OF ESCAPE

It does not matter what circumstance we are in, God before the foundation of the world has already made a way out. All we have to do is to discern the way out that God has established for us. God has given us the instinct to be able to protect ourselves and we have the ability to see where our escape is.

When we find ourselves in a tempting situation, we are to go to God and ask for grace in our time of need. Before we get to the point of giving in to temptation, we have the promise that He will give us the strength and or the means to get out of the situation. At the right time, He will give us the power to overcome temptation.

Our ability to escape temptation is not the only way God provides us escape. He also provides a way to escape in dangerous situations or circumstances.

Examples:

Escape Through Warnings

Bob and Barb were sleeping in their home, when they heard a tornado warning. Quickly, they went to the basement to wait out the storm. Most of their house was destroyed, but they were safe in the basement. Bob and Barb also had knowledge of the best procedure to take when there is a tornado. Bob and Barb had an escape plan along with previous knowledge.

A Simple 'No'

Adam and Eve could have just said no to the devil and sometimes a very simple way to escape is to just say "No".

Look Away

David could have looked the other way from Bethsheba and this was his way of escape which he ignored.

Keep Quiet

Samson should have kept his mouth shut.

Anna's Safe Choice

Anna was making up a physical education class that she missed the previous week on a Saturday morning. The building was almost completely deserted. When she left the class, she had to walk down a long corridor to get to her car. Toward the end of the hall a man that she had never seen before was yelling and motioning to her to come and enter a room with him. She had an eerie feeling about this. She decided not to pass by him. There was another hallway to her right with an outside door at the end. Anna also saw a group of students talking beyond the door. She chose to escape the situation without a confrontation and exited the building by the side door. This was a wise way of accessing a way of escape.

LAW 26

The Law of Success
Joshua 1:8

8 This book of the law shall not depart out of thy mouth; but thou shalt meditate therein day and night, that thou mayest observe to do according to all that is written therein: for then thou shalt make thy way prosperous, and then thou shalt have good success.

THE LAW OF SUCCESS

Christians are admonished to meditate on the Word of God, day and night. That is the only way to be assured of good (or Godly) success. There is success identified by the world's system, but true success comes only by meditating on the Word, being in God's purpose and in his specific assignment for us.

Examples:

Abraham's Obedience

Abraham was obedient to God's Word. God told him to sacrifice his son and he was going to do it, but God sent a ram and told him to sacrifice the ram instead. Because of his obedience to the Word of

God, God said He would make great nations from him. Eventually, Jesus was born from his bloodline.

Paul's Knowledge

Paul was a student of Mosaic law. After he accepted Christ, he was able to use his understanding of the Mosaic law as well as spiritual laws to persuade others to come to Christ. He was successful in the assignment he had been given.

LAW 27

The Law of Work

2 Thessalonians 3:10

10 For even when we were with you, this we commanded you, that if any would not work, neither should he eat.
11 For we hear that there are some which walk among you disorderly, working not at all, but are busybodies.
12 Now them that are such we command and exhort by our Lord Jesus Christ, that with quietness they work, and eat their own bread.

THE LAW OF WORK

Scriptures require us to work, to be productive, to be fruitful and to multiply. Laziness, idle hands, slothfulness, is frowned upon and if we fail to work, we should not expect to eat.

Because we are made in God's image, an important part of us is to work. He also tells us to be productive and take care of the things on this earth.

We all have been given gifts and are expected to use them. Romans 12:6-8 On top of that we are to work with all our heart as we are doing it for the Lord. Colossians 3:23

Examples:

Short Cuts Cause Problems

Sheila has been employed by a certain company for several years. She is very conscientious in her employment but as time progressed she has learned short cuts. She began to take every opportunity, not to work. Sheila began to take extended breaks, have lengthy conversations with other employees, any and every way to avoid work including shifting her assignments to others. Her supervisors became aware, called her in and gave her a firm warning.

Laid Off

Dan was laid off from his job. He was eligible for unemployment pay for which he applied and received. A condition for continued receipt of unemployment checks was for Dan to regularly seek employment. He became accustomed to relaxing at home, watching sports on TV and stopped looking for a job. His checks were suspended.

Work Not Done

Marcel was a community college coach and physical education teacher. He is able to retire at 60 years of age. He could stay home, travel, and play golf. Though Marcel is able to do those things, he decides his work is not done. He coaches a Little League Baseball team, teaches a Bible study in a prison, and serves on several community committees. The Law of Work covers more than how a person makes their living. Marcel found many ways to be valuable to others and remains productive sometimes even working harder than before.

LAW 28

The Law of Bearability
1 Corinthians 10:13

There hath no temptation taken you but such as is common to man: but God is faithful, who will not suffer you to be tempted above that ye are able; but will with the temptation also make a way to escape, that ye may be able to bear it.

THE LAW OF BEARABILITY

Father God, knowing all things, knows what He has deposited in us, therefore knowing our level of bearability. He therefore, will not allow any more on you than you are able to bear. He determines the limits on what comes upon you.

No one knows you better than God. He even knew you when you were conceived. God has infinite knowledge. There is nothing that He does not know. He knows our every thought, desire, and action. He also has control of everything. Nothing happens if He does not allow it. So, He knows what we can take, though sometimes we ask "Why me, God? I cannot take it anymore." But He knows what we can take and will not put on us more than we can withstand.

Examples:

<u>Can Make You Stronger</u>

A person experiences neglect and abuse. They could make all kinds of bad choices. Instead, they let the bad times in their life make them grow stronger. They make something of their life and get their master's degree in nursing. They endured and overcame their circumstances.

<u>Overcame Poverty</u>

Ben Carson lived in the projects. He lived in extreme poverty but his mother stressed the importance of his education. He became a famous surgeon and an important political figure. There is a movie about him called "Gifted Hands: The Ben Carson Story".

<u>A Single Mother's Plight</u>

A single mother has a special needs child; she also has a demanding job and receives little or no support from family. Many ask the question, how can she do it? She realizes that it cannot be done in her own strength, but God has given her the grace to be able to bear it.

LAW 29

The Law of Service

Galatians 5:13

13 For, brethren, ye have been called unto liberty; only use not liberty for an occasion to the flesh, but by love serve one another.

THE LAW OF SERVICE

The emphasis to believers is not to have total focus on oneself, but more so on how we can be of service to others. If we do so, we combine the Law of Sowing and Reaping with the Law of Service, and we receive a corresponding harvest of service from others.

When we serve others, we are showing them love. As we love others, we also show love to God. Through service, we show our relationship with God and being obedient to His Word. Proof of your relationship plays out in service to others. Service that we are expected to do should be done with your whole heart and to the best of your ability.

Examples:

Hospitality as Service

Abraham saw three strangers approaching. He ran out to meet them. They turned out to be angels. The people of Israel were encouraged to show hospitality to travelers. They washed their feet and fed them.

Mary and Martha

Mary and Martha were followers and friends of Jesus and His disciples. They let Jesus stay at their house and served Him and those traveling with Him. The women fed them, washed their feet, gave them a place to stay, and spent time with them. When Mary sat at Jesus' feet, while Martha stayed busy taking care of the household, Martha got upset. In this case, Mary did the right thing, so we know time and communication is another way to serve and please God.

Caring for the Hungry

Ed is a limo driver in Miami. During his shift, he sees homeless people throughout the city. He purchases food for the homeless and delivers it to them. When he sees an opportunity to help others, he steps up. He also helps in a teen center as a mentor. Kindness and serving others is an everyday part of who he is. He seeks no recognition or reward for the things he does, in fact, few people know.

Finding Favor

Norma receives great joy in serving others. When she has guests at her house, she waits on them hand and foot because she enjoys blessing others and likes to extend hospitality. Because of her service to others she receives favor everywhere she goes.

Joy in Serving

Brad had a successful construction job. He eventually realized that though the money was good, he was not feeling satisfied. He decided to change jobs and work in a nursing home. He always loved talking and caring for the elderly. Though his income was less he found fulfillment in serving the elderly and he found happiness and meaning in his work.

LAW 30
The Law of Reputation and Character
Proverbs 22:1

A good name is rather to be chosen than great riches, and loving favour rather than silver and gold.

THE LAW OF REPUTATION AND CHARACTER

Reputation is what people say about you, but character is who you are, and what you do, when (you think) no one is watching. God looks on the heart, and He determines and judges us based upon the intent of our hearts.

A good reputation should be maintained so that you can achieve success. A good name glorifies God and opens up opportunities to do good. If you are rich, you can feed others. If you have a good reputation, it is easier for you to evangelize.

A person can have a reputation as an individual, a company, organization, government, or a country. A good reputation means that people think well of you and that you are trustworthy and they want to work with you.

The Biblical meaning of reputation is a person who carries the characteristics of God. The person pursues righteousness, faith, love, kindness, faithfulness, gentleness, and self-control. Galatians 5:22-23.

Examples:

Job's Trials

Job had a good name and even when he lost everything, he maintained his faith and his good name. When his trials were over, he still had his good name.

Paul's Discipline

Paul said in Acts 24, that because he believes there will be a resurrection *"I will exercise and discipline myself (mortifying my body, deadening my carnal affection, bodily appetites, and worldly desires, endeavoring in all respects) to have a clear (unshaken and blameless) conscience, void of offense toward God and toward men.* Amplified Version

Poor Credit

Jane doesn't pay her bills on time. Jane, because her reputation for credit worthiness is poor, has made it difficult for her to buy a car and to be creditworthy.

Generational Reputation

Edward lost his job and was frantically looking for another because he has a family to support. He saw a help wanted ad and went to interview for the job. During the course of the interview, he was asked about his parents and he mentioned his father's name. The interviewer was familiar with Edward's father and his father's reputation. Because Edward's father had such an outstanding reputation, Edward was hired on the spot.

Ethical Business Practices

A business owner neglects to fully disclose the costs for a service. The service cost more than what the customer expected and as a result she writes negative things about his business on Facebook and other media. If he had followed procedures, he may have gotten good ratings and increased business.

Cheating on Taxes

Bob cheats on his taxes, gets caught and his reputation is damaged. He may even go to jail.

Law 31
The Law of Waste and Want
Luke 15

And he said, A certain man had two sons:
And the younger of them said to his father, Father, give me the portion of goods that falleth to me. And he divided unto them his living.
And not many days after the younger son gathered all together, and took his journey into a far country, and there wasted his substance with riotous living.
And when he had spent all, there arose a mighty famine in that land; and he began to be in want.
And he went and joined himself to a citizen of that country; and he sent him into his fields to feed swine.
And he would fain have filled his belly with the husks that the swine did eat: and no man gave unto him.
And when he came to himself, he said, How many hired servants of my father's have bread enough and to spare, and I perish with hunger!
I will arise and go to my father, and will say unto him, Father, I have sinned against heaven, and before thee,
And am no more worthy to be called thy son: make me as one of thy hired servants.
And he arose, and came to his father. But when he was yet a great way off, his father saw him, and had compassion, and ran, and fell on his neck, and kissed him.

THE LAW OF WASTE AND WANT

It does not matter how much you or I may have. If we are wasteful, there will come a day when we will find ourselves in want. The more we waste, the less we are going to have. This is true for the believer as well as for the unbeliever.

God is not a God of waste. He does not waste anything. According to His design, throughout nature nothing is wasted. He does not waste our experiences. He uses them for our growth. He doesn't waste the heartache we experience. He uses them to make us strong. John 6:12

A person may waste things other than just material resources. They may also waste talents, spiritual gifts, time, attention to others, and opportunities. If we do not use our talents and spiritual gifts, they will wither away. We can never be who we were meant to be. Time wasted can never be regained. Think of the people you wished you had given time and attention to and now they are gone and it is too late.

Examples:

Lot's wife was given an opportunity to escape the destruction of Sodom and Gomorrah. The only condition was that she could not look back. She looked back and she wasted her opportunity for escape.

"He who is faithful in a little, is also faithful in much..."
Luke 16:10

Wasted Money

Amanda gets a paycheck and eats out every day instead of getting groceries. When rent is due, she doesn't have the full amount to pay the rent.

Wasted Time

Each Saturday, a man goes golfing. His mother has been ill and he tells her he will visit next week. During the week, his mother passes away. The time he spent golfing could have been spent with his mother. He wasted his last opportunity to be with her before she passed away.

Wasted Food

A family has a rule of not eating any leftovers. As a result they throw away tons of food. Both parents are laid off, now they can hardly buy food. Was their refusal to eat leftovers a waste because now they find themselves in want?

LAW 32
The Law of Worship
John 4: 23, 24

23 But the hour is coming, and now is, when the true worshipers will worship the father in spirit and truth, for such the father seeks to worship him.
24 God is spirit, and those who worship him must worship in spirit and truth.

THE LAW OF WORSHIP

God is a Spirit, and they that worship Him, must (absolutely) worship Him in Spirit and in Truth. It does not matter what formalities we may be going through in our worship services. If worship is not done in Spirit and in Truth, based upon The Law of Worship, God does not receive it. It does not matter how quietly or loudly we worship, if it is not done in Spirit and in Truth it is not acceptable to our Heavenly Father.

We are created to bring God glory, but this does not happen just by uttering words or singing songs. Worship must come from the Spirit. I Chronicles 16

Examples:

<u>David's Song</u>

David played a lyre and other instruments to praise God. He wrote the Psalms and with his beautiful words, he praised God before all the assembly. I Chronicles 29

David's joy and passion in life was to worship God. He led others to long be a part of the worship and bring God into fellowship with the people. Longing comes from the spirit. The more David worshiped God the closer he became to being a man after God's own heart. He learned to love what God loved.

<u>Worship Through Service</u>

A person glorifies God by giving Him praise not only with our words but with our hearts. A couple collects food to give to the homeless. By serving others, we are praising God with our actions.

<u>People May Worship Differently</u>

Jakes likes the lively service with lots of loud music, clapping, and 'Amens'. His wife, Jan, prefers a quiet dignified reserved service. They are having difficulty finding a church home suitable for both. They both feel that their preferred way of worship is that which is received by God. Who's right?

The Widow's Mite

A widow had two mites which was a very small amount. Jesus recognized the gift even though it was not monetarily very valuable because it was all she had. Jesus considered it to be a great gift and an amazing act of worship. She showed her devotion and love for God by her actions.

Paul and Silas Singing in Prison

Paul and Silas were put in a Philippi prison for being a public nuisance and were flogged and beaten. Their jailors were unable to stop them from worshiping. At midnight, they sang and praised God. There was an earthquake and their chains were broken and the prison door was opened. Their jailors did not stop them.

Philip's Ministry

Philip grew up living in the streets of St. Louis. Even in his early teens, he became involved in a life of crime running with other young men in his community. By the time he was in his twenties, he was convicted of armed robbery and sentenced to prison. During his time in prison, he became a Christian and dedicated his life to Christ. He studied and worshiped and eventually gained an early parole. After his release, he became a street preacher ministering to street people and doing drug counseling and most of all continued to worship in every way.

LAW 33
The Law of Forfeiture
Ezra 10:8

and that if any one did not come within three days, by order of the officials and the elders all property should be forfeited, and he himself banned from the congregation of the exiles.

THE LAW OF FORFEITURE

If Ezra sent the Israelites an order to appear before them and they did not come within three days, a penalty of forfeiting one's property was given to them. Forfeiture means that there is a loss or liability for consequences of a breach of contract or offense. If we damage anyone else's property, we are required to make restitution. There are consequences for the things we do.

Examples:

Bill of Rights

The United States Bill of Rights says that forfeiture of life, liberty or property can not be made without due process of law.

Embezzlement

A man that embezzled money from a business must make restitution as prescribed by law. He will need to forfeit his property to pay the money back.

Right to Vote

John, recently released from prison, now realizes that a felony conviction not only forfeited his freedom for a period of time, but he also forfeited temporarily or permanently his right to vote, bear arms, get federal loans and many other opportunities.

Drunk Driver

Bill, a physician, had been drinking. He was on call at the hospital. He thought he would not be discovered; he had gotten away with it before. This particular night there was an accident. Bill was called in to the hospital. The patient required delicate surgery to save his life. Bill should have passed on doing the surgery, but he didn't think the few drinks had impaired him. He performed the surgery and the surgery did not go well. The patient died. The patient may have died anyway, but the patient's family sued and there was an investigation. It was discovered that Bill had been drinking. Bill had to forfeit his medical license. He lost his malpractice insurance and his job. He had to sell his home to cover what costs the insurance did not pay. Bill forfeited most of what he had worked for by his actions.

LAW 34

The Law of Imputation

Romans 4:18-25

18 Who against hope believed in hope, that he might become the father of many nations, according to that which was spoken, So shall thy seed be.
19 And being not weak in faith, he considered not his own body now dead, when he was about an hundred years old, neither yet the deadness of Sarah's womb:
20 He staggered not at the promise of God through unbelief; but was strong in faith, giving glory to God;
21 And being fully persuaded that, what he had promised, he was able also to perform.
22 And therefore it was imputed to him for righteousness.
23 Now it was not written for his sake alone, that it was imputed to him;
24 But for us also, to whom it shall be imputed, if we believe on him that raised up Jesus our Lord from the dead;
25 Who was delivered for our offences, and was raised again for our justification.

THE LAW OF IMPUTATION

Imputation is defined as the action or process of ascribing righteousness, guilt, etc. to someone by virtue of a similar quality in another. (Oxford) As we are using it, it also applies to an association with another.

The consequences of what I do and what I may fail to do, do not end with me. It also impacts or imputes to those who are under my control. Our sin was also imputed on Jesus, who paid the price for our sin and his righteousness was imputed to us.

Imputation is involved from top to bottom in relationships as well as bottom to top. The actions of an employer or parent for example is imputed to the employee or child. The employee or child's actions are also imputed to the employer or the parent. Relationships are intertwined.

Examples:

<u>Sins of the World Upon Jesus</u>

The sins of the world were imputed on Jesus and through His suffering gave people of the world a pathway to being saved from death. Our sins were imputed onto Jesus and His suffering made it possible for Salvation to be imputed onto us.

Employers Liability

Joe was a truck driver for XYZ company. One day while traveling from one drop off location to another he failed to stop for a stop sign and crashed into another vehicle. The other driver was seriously injured and sued Joe and his employer. Joe's negligence was imputed to his employer based upon the employer employee relationship.

LAW 35
The Law of Brokenness
Matthew 21:44

And whosoever shall fall on this stone shall be broken: but on whomsoever it shall fall, it will grind him to powder.

THE LAW OF BROKENNESS

One must be broken in order to be made whole. God is looking for those who have a broken and contrite spirit. Only those who have been broken can be used to their fullest. From God's perspective when a person is considered to be broken, a person is so crushed by the sin and darkness of the world, that there is no place to turn but to God. When that occurs there is a surrender to God where he can then be used by God and be made whole.

Examples:

Peter's Denial

After Jesus was arrested, Peter denied his relationship with Jesus three times. When he realized what he had done for fear of being arrested too, he had a broken heart. Peter's faith was made strong. He became a powerful evangelist and the Christian faith was built upon Peter's faith.

Salvation Story

Ann was raised in the church. She sought Jesus, but couldn't seem to accept Christ in the way she needed to. She felt broken because she knew she should already be a Christian. She went to a retreat at Turkey Run Park in Indiana. That day the preacher said the perfect words that could touch her heart and she laid all of her heart at the feet of Jesus and she became a Christian.

Tom's Affair

Tom was having an affair with a married woman and justified it because he loves her and she loves him. Tom doesn't see that it is never alright to have an affair with a married person. No matter what his friends advised, Tom will probably not turn from the sin unless he is broken.

Drug Dealer

Robert had been what he considered to be a successful drug dealer with plenty of cash, homes, cars, jewelry, and fast women. He was caught in a drug bust, convicted and sentenced to 20 years in prison. After losing it all his pride, arrogance, and self-sufficiency were broken. He humbled himself in his cell and accepted Jesus as Savior and Lord. He realized that if he had not been broken that he probably would still be lost in sin.

LAW 36
The Law of Truth
John 14:6

Jesus saith unto him, I am the way, the truth, and the life: no man cometh unto the Father, but by me.

THE LAW OF TRUTH

The only real truth is what comes by and through the Word of God. His truth is absolute, while all other so-called truth is relative at best. The truth we are talking about here is the truth that comes from God's voice and His Spirit.

We are taught to walk in truth and faithfulness. By walking in truth, we are obedient to God. The more we walk in truth the closer we walk with God and become like Him.

Examples:

<u>**Truth Rejected**</u>

When Moses, who was providing truth, went up into Mount Sinai and came down from Mt. Sinai, the people became impatient because he had been gone for 40 days and they turned to idols. Those that sided with idolatry were slain because they rejected truth.

Truth Not Always Taught in Church

Some churches will emphasize good works over being saved by Grace.

A prominent television figure will profess to be a Christian, but follows a guru that practices ancient religions. Many people listen to her because of who she is, but she is leading them down the wrong path and untruth.

Cancer Diagnosis

Linda goes for her routine physical exam. She is told she has terminal cancer and only expected to live 6 months. The facts of her situation are dismal but she holds true to the truth of God's Word 'By His stripes we are healed', which is found in Isaiah 53:5 and I Peter 2:24.

Facts say I am weak but truth says I am strong. Facts say I am poor but truth says I am rich. Facts say I am sick but truth says I am well.

All of the Laws of Life are spiritual truths.

LAW 37

The Law of Direction
Proverbs 3:5-6

5 Trust in the Lord with all your heart, and do not rely on your own understanding. 6 In all thy ways acknowledge him, and he shall direct thy paths.

THE LAW OF DIRECTION

When we acknowledge God in everything that we do, He has committed himself to direct our paths. We will not get off course. Whatever decisions you make in life, getting a new job, finding a place to live, choosing a spouse, etc. consult God. He will show you the way and also remove obstacles. Life can be challenging. Making foolish decisions makes life even more challenging. God speaks to us through His Word. Following God's Word helps you avoid poor decisions. We need to focus on what He is telling us and listen to His Spirit to guide us.

Examples:

Finding a Wife

Abraham sent his servant to find his son Isaac a wife. His servant prayed and Rebekah came to the well where he was watering his camel. God let him know this was the woman to be Isaac's wife.

Making Decisions on Your Own

A woman was in a bad place with God. She was at a time in her life when she wanted to be married. She did not pray about it. She only went with her feelings and married a man who abused her and ran around with other women. Following her own direction caused her many heartaches and difficult times.

Forgiveness

A man could not forgive a friend for stealing his girlfriend. God's Word said to forgive and you will be forgiven. His life was filled with bitterness. God directs us to be forgiving. Psalm 32:8

LAW 38

The Law of Completion
Phillipians 1:6

And I am sure that he who began a good work in you will bring it to completion at the day of Jesus Christ.

THE LAW OF COMPLETION

God will always complete what he has started. He never leaves anything or anyone of His incomplete; for He is a God of completion.

God's creation is perfect and complete.

God knows a person when a person is conceived. He knows everything the person will do and could do. He allows situations and puts people in their life for them to fulfill their destiny.

Examples:

God's Timing

A woman in her 70's becomes a writer and does a lot in her life for good. She can see that all her experiences in life have led her to this time. Sometimes, she wonders why this didn't happen earlier, but God's timing is perfect.

God's Promise

Jesus was sent to earth 100% man and 100% God. He was sent to earth to die for our sins so that we can have eternal life. It was hard. He was a man who felt the burden of every sin of man; all the sin already committed, all present sin, and all future sin. He felt the pain of betrayal, every lash of the whip and the thorns digging into His flesh. He died and in three days arose from the grave. God's promise was completed in Jesus.

Terry's Purpose

It had been revealed to Terry by scripture, prophecy, and spiritual dreams that he was going to have a platform to reach the entire world with the Gospel. Presently, Terry has only 10 people in his weekly Bible class. He holds to his faith that God will complete what he promised to do.

LAW 39

The Law of Patterns

Titus 2:7

In all things shewing thyself a pattern of good works: in doctrine shewing uncorrupted, gravity, sincerity,

THE LAW OF PATTERNS

Everything God made he made according to a pattern. Nothing created was made helter skelter without a system or design. Trees, grass, flowers, and all of creation have a pattern and the same is true with our lives.

As God created the world, He followed a pattern as laid out in Genesis. First, He made an announcement by saying 'And God said'. Secondly, He gave the command with the words 'let there be'. Next, He gave a report 'and it was so'. Then, He evaluated what He made by saying 'And God said it was good'. Lastly, He gave a framework- 'And there was evening and morning'. We can see this pattern played out in other stories throughout the Bible. Such as in the story of Noah.

When we see a Spiritual truth in the Bible and see that it is repeated throughout the Bible in both the New and Old Testament, we see a pattern in the way God operates. All the Laws of Life are examples of the Law of Patterns.

What we are to be is written in a book according to God's design for our life. Psalm 40:7 Jesus followed the design written for Him. When a person operates contrary to the design God has set for him, he will have troubles in his life.

Examples:

<u>Edward's Understanding</u>

Edward is now 80 years of age. In looking back over his life, he sees he would go up in his career just so far, but everytime he got involved in a certain activity he would begin to come down in his career. In this late stage of his life, he finally sees the pattern and the reason for reversal of progress.

The Seasons

A year is made up of seasons. How the seasons are shown depends on the climate where they live. We have winter, spring, summer, fall and we know this will happen every year. Likewise, we also have seasons in our life with times of rest, growth, achievement, etc. When we recognize the seasons, we can be more productive. It is one of the patterns God has set for us.

Study of Behavior

In the study of behavior, a reinforced behavior will increase whether the behavior is given a negative or positive reinforcement. A behavior that gets no reinforcement will decrease according to the pattern which has been established by God.

Diet and Calories

A person who eats more calories than they burn is going to gain weight. A person who eats fewer calories than they burn will lose weight. A balance has to be maintained to stay at the same weight. Any diet plan you try doesn't matter; it still comes down to the pattern of calories in and calories out.

LAW 40
The Law of Suffering
2 Timothy 3:12

Yea, and all that will live godly in Christ Jesus shall suffer persecution

THE LAW OF SUFFERING

The world or the systems of this world will hate you. If you are friends of the world, the world loves you, but we then become enemies of God. In a time where we are receiving applause and accolades from the world, we better take heed and examine our Christian walk. The world may hate us and we may as well expect it.

Suffering is defined in Webster's dictionary to endure death, pain, or distress, to sustain loss or damage, , and to be subject to disability or handicap. Romans 5:12 defines suffering as a product of the fall, a consequence of human sin against God. Part of suffering comes from living in a world that is sinful and broken and some from our own sin.

Suffering is not necessarily a bad thing. From suffering we learn to endure, gain strength, and push us toward hope given to us by God's Spirit. Romans 8:1-17.

Examples:

Persecution of Christians

Not too long ago in Nigeria, a whole farming village was murdered for being Christian.

Christians in China and many places throughout the world are persecuted.

Persecution in the Media

Today in the USA, people in certain industries ridicule Christian values because it exposes their sin. Sin is sin regardless of the offender, but there is no condemnation in Christ. A mature Christian should feel the same with no condemnation toward them.

Ruined Reputation in the Media

A Christian teenage boy was at a pro-life rally in Washington D.C. The media showed the teen face to face with an elderly man and portrayed him as threatening the man. The news made the teenager look bad as he just stood calmly before the man. The boy would suffer the impact of the lie told in the media throughout his life as he applied for jobs and lived out his life. The truth was later revealed that the man was the one threatening and confronting him. The teen was just holding his ground and keeping his cool. The boy's reputation suffered. Ultimately, there were lawsuits that cleared the boys reputation and he was awarded a large financial judgement.

LAW 41
The Law of Foreseeability
Proverbs 22:3

A prudent man foreseeth the evil, and hideth himself: but the simple pass on, and are punished.

THE LAW OF FORESEEABILITY

This law says to the believer that we should see trouble and evil from afar off. God gives us foreseeability when it comes time for us to do things, because they may lead us into doing things that are not from God.

Foreseeability can be a legal term. The law asks how likely it was that a person could have anticipated the potential or actual results of their actions. It is used in contract and tort law. The court asks how likely an ordinary person in the same circumstances would have reasonably acted in the same way.

Proverbs 22 says that we are given foreseeability in our circumstances to avoid trouble.

One operating under foreseeability sees trouble from afar off and is not caught by surprise as the world is.

Examples:

<u>Body Tells of Health Concerns</u>

Mark sees his wife is not feeling well. He has a feeling that this is something more than a cold. He encourages her to see a doctor. She says it will pass and she will go after she finishes a work project. Time passes and she finally goes to the doctor. The doctor told her she has stage 4 lung cancer. if she had adhered to the Law of Foreseeability sooner she may have avoided the problems she will be dealing with now.

<u>Coming Storm</u>

The sky turns dark. The barometer is dropping. A man feels the coming storm in the air. He prepares for the storm.

<u>Mother's Intervention</u>

A son is making a habit of sneaking in after curfew. The mother intervenes before the son makes a serious mistake with long term consequences.

Uneasy Feeling

Shelby was invited by a friend to go to Amitabha Stupa Peace Garden in Sedona, Arizona to go on a hike. Her friend invited her to the garden because she is a spiritual person. When Shelby got to the beginning of the trail, God impressed on her not to go. She told her friend she would wait for her there. Shelby later found that there was an altar with relics, objects blessed with rituals, many idols, etc. It is a Budhist's worship site. If she had gone down the trail, she would have sorely regretted it. Her friend was upset with her because she thought Shelby should be open to all spirits. Shelby plainly told her that there is only one spirit she wants and that is the Holy Spirit.

Foreseeability in Dreams

Shelby is a woman who is very much into prayer and the power of the Holy Spirit. One night, she had a dream that her brother, Fred and her sister, Betty Ann were in coffins. God impressed upon her to pray. There was a snow storm and they were traveling home. The snow was coming down hard. They came up on a snow plow that was backing up and the backup lights on the truck did not work. They could not see the truck and ran into the truck. Because of the Law of Foreseeability, she had been praying and perhaps because of her prayers, they were spared. Another time there was tornadic activity and she dreamt that her sister and brother in-law were in coffins. God impressed upon her to pray. The tornado hit their farm. A wall fell and pinned the brother-in-law in something like a tunnel. Her sister was taking the children into the cellar. When going into the cellar, she usually would run her hand along a pipe for balance. This time she could not do so because both children were in her arms. An electric wire fell against the house and electricity ran through the pipes. She would have been electrocuted. In both cases, family members may have been spared because of the law of foreseeability and the power of prayer.

Oncoming Death

For a time, Shelby worked in a nursing home, Shelby would be given the foreseeability of someone's death. God would impress upon her to see the person before their death to lead them to the Lord.

LAW 42
Spiritual Law and Principles
Romans 14:13

Therefore let us not pass judgement on one another any longer, but rather decide never to put a stumbling block or hindrance in the way of a brother.

LAWS OF SPIRITUAL LIFE AND PRINCIPLES

A principle is a fundamental truth. It is not absolute and is relative to circumstances. A law of life, or spiritual law, on the other hand is an absolute Divine rule that governs the consequences of our actions and is composed of a body of established principles.

Examples:

Modesty in Dress

Jane has always been known, even before she became a Christian, as a fashionable and sometimes provocative dresser. Oftentimes, she wears outfits that make the women in the church uncomfortable because they are somewhat revealing. Some of the ladies have decided to approach Jane in love and discuss with her the principle of modesty in dress.

Lifestyle Example

John and his wife are teachers in their church assembly. They enjoy going to a wholesome movie from time to time. They were in line on this occasion, when some babes in the faith were driving by and saw them in the movie line. The new Christians looked at them with disappointment. John and his wife are now evaluating whether they should be going to movies of any kind. It is not a sin to go to a movie. The point of this example is that the less mature Christian may lose their way if they see mature Christians in what they perceive to be questionable activities. The couple in this example might discuss this together and decide the best thing to do. Your testimony is more important than a movie or any other activity. A second point is that as Christians we don't live under condemnation so that would be another lesson for the less mature Christian to learn.

Therefore let us not pass judgement on one another any longer, but rather decide never to put a stumbling block or hindrance in the way of a brother. Romans 14:13

A Glass of Wine

A woman likes to enjoy an occasional glass of wine. She rarely drinks, not because she doesn't want to or thinks a simple glass of wine is wrong, but she would not want someone who may later have a problem with drinking to use her as an example to become a heavy drinker.

Therefore, if food makes my brother stumble, I will never eat meat, lest I make my brother stumble. I Corinthians 8:13

LAW 43

Spiritual Law and the Prophetic
Amos 3:7

Surely the Lord God will do nothing, but he revealeth his secret unto his servants the prophets.

SPIRITUAL LAW AND THE PROPHETIC

A true prophetic word (without exceptions) incorporates one or more Laws of Life. A prophetic word is predicting what will happen in the future.

Examples:

<u>Inconsistent with Scripture</u>

Elder Johnson, in a recent church service prophesied that the date and hour of the return of our Lord and Savior Jesus Christ has been revealed to him. This prophecy is not received by the elders and members of the congregation. It conflicts with scripture which says to us that no man knows the day or hour of His return.

Word Consistent with Scripture

At another service, a prophetic word is uttered that we are in the last of the last days and even more perilous times are forthcoming. This word is received by the assembly under the Law of Foreseeability.

"For no prophecy was ever produced by the will of man, but men spoke from God as they were carried along by the Holy Spirit." (II Peter 1:21)

LAW 44

Law of Overstepping
Ephesians 6:4

And, ye fathers, provoke not your children to wrath: but bring them up in the nurture and admonition of the Lord.

THE LAW OF OVERSTEPPING

Overstepping means to pass beyond or exceed a limit or standard. The person extends themselves beyond their limit of authority. If a person is asked to do something immoral, even though the person may have authority over that person, by asking them to do something illegal they have overstepped.

Examples:

Downloaded App

It was suggested on the news that we download an App on our phone so they could trace all the people we are in contact with because of the Covid-19 virus. That suggestion leads to the possibility of overstepping.

Parent's Authority

Parents are authority figures for their children and can sometimes abuse their authority thereby overstepping. When parents overstep their authority they bring themselves under judgement. Overstepping applies to every aspect of life when authority is abused.

Jake and Nancy are two very strict parents. They have a militaristic approach to parenting which includes severe corporal punishment. A neighbor complains to local child authorities and the parents are investigated and charged with child abuse. They had overstepped their God given authority as parents and are now being held accountable.

Coach Endangers Health

A high school football coach is obsessed with winning and insists on strenuous training for his players which includes practicing in unbearable heat. One of his players during practice had a heat stroke and was hospitalized. The coach was held accountable by authorities because he overstepped his authority.

LAW 45

The Law of Provocation
Ephesians 6:4

4 And, ye fathers, provoke not your children to wrath: but bring them up in the nurture and admonition of the Lord.

THE LAW OF PROVOCATION

We are not to provoke our children to wrath. Provocation can come in the form of rage, exasperation, or vexing, to name a few, and does not end with our children. We are not to provoke anyone.

There are three types of provocation. One is an unintentional action which causes another to react. The second is an intentional action. The third is malevolent provocation which is an intentional action given to cause anger or even violence.

Examples:

Harsh Discipline

A son makes some bad choices. The parents in disciplining him are unduly harsh. The son runs away and they never hear from him again and they never know what happened to him. The son's actions may have been the result of his parents overstepping their authority.

Negative Long-Term Consequences

A student has a defiant attitude. She was in the school hall during class time. She is stopped by a teacher that has had enough of her attitude. Being a teacher, he should have had more constraint, but he used foul language and yelled at her. The student returned the yelling and language. The student was expelled from school and eventually dropped out of school. Both provoked the other. There were negative long-term consequences for the student. The student's version of the story was not believed. She had a pattern of defiance and bad temper. Both parties may have overstepped their boundaries. The teacher using foul language overstepped his authority to do so and the girl overstepped by not respecting the teacher.

LAW 46
The Law of Delegability and Non-Delegability
Colossians 3:19-21

*Husbands, love your wives, and be not be bitter against them.
Children obey your parents in all things: for this is well pleasing unto the Lord.
Fathers, provoke not your children to anger, lest they be discouraged.*

THE LAW OF DELEGABILITY AND NON-DELEGABILITY

There are some activities under The Law of Accountability and Responsibility that we cannot, according to the Word of God, delegate to anyone else. There are some responsibilities that cannot be shifted to another. The role of a parent, spouse, son or daughter should not be delegated to another.

There are times when we should delegate. God told Moses in Numbers 11:17 in reference to leadership "delegate; let other men share the burden with you so that you don't bear it alone."

Examples:

A Man's Prayers

Jerry was in constant pain. He and his wife, Peggy would call their daughter to pray for his pain. He was relieved for a while and then his pain would return. He could not understand why God had not healed him.

God led Jerry's daughter to write her parents a letter. In the letter, she told him that God said, "Jerry, you know I hear your prayers too." Jerry took this to heart and he began praying himself. God healed him. Jerry had been delegating his prayers to his daughter instead of praying for himself. He did not need to rely on the faith of others, while his own faith could make him whole.

Attention to Children

Tom and Susie have 5 children. Tom works hard to provide for his family and is of the opinion that they get sufficient attention to make up for the fact that he has little time for them. He is trying to delegate a duty no one else can fill.

Duty as Father

A father has been in prison and he has been told by other inmates and his prison counselor that there is little to nothing that he can do for his children while he is confined. As he submits himself to God, he studies Scripture and learns that his duty as a father is not suspended and there is much he can do while confined to be a responsible father.

LAW 47

Law of Contamination
1 Corinthians 5:6

Your glorying is not good. Know ye not that a little leaven leaveneth the whole lump?

THE LAW OF CONTAMINATION

It has been said that a rotten apple will spoil the entire barrel. The same is true of human relationships. The wrong person can negatively impact an entire group.

Bad company can corrupt good manners. If one continues to be around and interact with bad company, it can have a negative effect and corrupt one's character.

For from within, out of the heart of men, proceed evil thoughts, adulteries, fornications, murders, thefts, covetousness, wickedness, deceit, lasciviousness, an evil eye, blasphemy, pride, foolishness: All these evil things come from within, and defile the man," Mark 7:20-23 Any time we let these things enter our lives, we open the door to contamination.

Examples:

Hummingbird Environment

Hummingbirds are territorial. They will not allow certain other birds to feed in their feeder because they will contaminate their food supply. If the water becomes contaminated, they will die.

Teen Hangs out with the Wrong Friends

A teenager hangs around with a group of friends. She enjoys them because she feels accepted. Some of them often tell lies to their parents about their activities. The girl also starts telling lies too and the others encourage her to do so. Sometimes, it seems easier to lie even when the truth wouldn't get them into trouble. Lying becomes a habit. It appears she has become contaminated by this group of friends.

Sex Outside of Marriage

Mental, emotional, physical and spiritual contamination occurs when there is sex outside of marriage or even thoughts of sex. In all cultures, there are many temptations. In modern times the exposure to sex is through tv, movies, our computers, and by people around us. The possibilities are endless and at your fingertips. Contamination is always around us. As Christians, we can have victory over it because of Jesus.

King David's Affair

King David loved God more than anything. He looked from his palace on Bathsheba and lusted after her. As a result, he had an affair with her and she got pregnant. He had her husband killed. Eventually, the child got sick and died. David came back to God. In this case, David became contaminated and contaminated those around him.

LAW 48

Law of Corruption
Matthew 7:17

Even so every good tree bringeth forth good fruit; but a corrupt tree bringeth forth evil fruit.

THE LAW OF CORRUPTION

Bad company can corrupt good manners. If one continues to surround and interact with bad company, it can have a negative effect and corrupt one's character.

Contamination and corruption are closely related. In many instances, they collaborate with one another.

Examples:

Alice's Boyfriend

Alice has a boyfriend who smokes. She takes a few puffs. He offers it to her again and she accepts. Eventually, she becomes a smoker which is bad for one's health.

Lude Pictures

Marianne has a friend who sends her lude pictures with funny jokes on social media. At first, she was shocked and should have asked her friend to stop sending them to her. Eventually, she accepts them and laughs. She also sends them to others and we now see a pattern of corruption being established. She may stay in that pattern until she is convicted of it.

LAW 49
Law of Confirmation
Romans 15:8

Now I say that Jesus Christ was a minister of the circumcision for the truth of God, to confirm the promises made unto the fathers:

THE LAW OF CONFIRMATION

God has committed himself under The Law of Notice and Warning, to make us aware of those things that present opportunity or danger to His people. He will not only give notice and warning, but will also provide confirmation of what one needs to know. Confirmation is the verification or proof of something.

Examples:

News Articles Confirm

A woman pays a lot of attention to the news and is aware that there is a possibility of a disease that could spread throughout the community. She is short on some supplies and it would be wise to stock up on some basics. She prepares accordingly. News articles keep confirming she was right.

Peace

Peace in your conscience is confirmation.

Signs in Environment

God puts up road signs. First, He puts the desire in your heart. Shelby, an artist, painted a mural on a wall in her home. She thought when I retire this is where I want to live. Then she looked on the internet for a place that would fit her painting and she found Sedona, Arizona. It became her dream to live there. Over the years, Shelby began having debilitating asthma symptoms. She was having difficulty breathing and was even rushed to the hospital near death. Her doctor found that she was allergic to black mold. Her doctor suggested she move to a healthier climate. She asked the doctor where she should live. The doctor told her Sedona, Arizona. Upon his recommendation, she visited Sedona and it matched the mural she had painted earlier. Everything fell into place and she moved to Sedona. Shelby had a vision of where she would love to live and had confirmation by a doctor that it would be a healthy place for her to live and now has fewer asthma problems.

LAW 50

Law of Provision
Philippians 4:19

But my God shall supply all your need according to his riches in glory by Christ Jesus. (KJV)

THE LAW OF PROVISION

Based upon the Law of Provision, whatever God has called you to do, He has already provided for because the provision for the thing that He has called you to do, is in the thing He has called you to do.

We should look to God for provision when we are in need and know that He has always provided adequate provision, when we need it.

Examples:

<u>**A Woman's Debt**</u>

Elijah, the Prophet, met a woman who was in debt. She was alone and could not feed her family. He told the woman to try and bring out jars and then she brought oil and the prophet blessed it and she became a seller of oil and was able to pay her debts and feed people around her and her children.

Health Restored

A present day example is about Lucas who fell in love with a woman that he believed God wanted him to marry. He was a man of faith and always tithed according to God's Will. The woman became seriously ill. The man felt he was led to give a little more which he did in obedience to God. The woman was restored to health and eventually fell in love with the man. It took awhile, but they were able to make a life together and because of the man's faith and sacrifice they lived a blessed, prosperous life. His obedience led to him receiving many blessings and his tithing led to being able to provide abundantly for his family.

Call to Ministry

Nathan, who had been a successful businessman, had accepted a call to the ministry. He was married with four children and his wife did not work outside of the home. They had a comfortable lifestyle. When he accepted the ministerial call, he expected everything to fall into place including finances for ministry and personal needs. His savings account dwindled down to almost nothing. He thought it was wise to take a part-time job. His finances seemed to have gotten worse. He finally decided that he was going to have to trust God to provide. He realized that a provision for what he was called to do was in what God had called him to do. He committed to full-time ministry, trusted God to provide, and he began to see his needs met and the abundant life that had been promised.

ADDENDUM

FRED M. MOSELY'S PERSONAL TESTIMONY

FRED M. MOSELY, J.D., LL.M

Former judge and author of *50 Laws of Life*

FRED'S TESTIMONY

I was born in 1944 in Birmingham, Alabama. The youngest of five children, my father was a coal miner and my mother did not work outside of the home. My modest lower middle-class home was Christian and my siblings and I were required to be active in the African Methodist Episcopal Church that we attended. Personally, I was on the usher board, in the junior choir and was president of the junior church. Our home was one of strict discipline tempered with love. My father was a hard worker and dependable provider. Whereas, my mother was a great cook, immaculate housekeeper and a kind hearted individual.

I attended public school in strictly segregated Birmingham and was a mediocre student until I reached the 5th grade. Obviously, someone, along with my parents and immediate family, was praying for me because I began to apply myself in school and became an "A" student and class president.

This positive pattern continued into high school where I finished as an honor student, student body president and senior class president. I was also a student athlete. Throughout my high school years, I remained active in church and was blessed with a scholarship to college, being the first in my family to go beyond secondary school.

My college years were truly blessed by the Lord, finishing with honors near the top of my class. During these years my commitment to my Savior had not waivered and though tempted as many college students are, I remained steadfast in the faith.

Upon graduation from Ohio Wilberforce University, I was blessed beyond my wildest imagination with an opportunity to attend law school in Ohio. I was accepted and my first racially integrated experience was in professional school. Being a minority, having come from segregated public schools, a family without a professional background, I was very intimidated, realizing that I truly needed the Lord's help. Continuing in Christian service as superintendent of Sunday school, church trustee and various other offices, I finished law school, earning the Juris Doctor and Master of Laws degrees, with honors.

The favor of the Lord was on my life and I received several attractive offers upon graduation, the most attractive of which were to serve as a clerk to a prestigious federal judge and the other with the U. S.

Justice Department as a trial attorney in the U. S. Justice Department Antitrust Division. I accepted the offer from the Justice Department and was privileged to speak to Ivy League lawyers in the Great Hall of the U. S. Justice Department.

I was the second African American hired by Antitrust in the history of the Department. My responsibilities in the position included but were not limited to investigating and prosecuting antitrust law violations within the United States of America. I traveled extensively, armed with my G-Man credentials, interfacing with high level corporate officials and senior partners of major law firms. I was assigned to some major investigations. Throughout this time period I remained faithful to my church.

Desiring more extensive trial experience, I resigned from Justice and accepted a position as an assistant district attorney in the State of Ohio. In this capacity, I tried numerous jury trials and handled vast number of pre-trials. Many of the high profile cases assigned to me received newspaper write-ups and I was interviewed on radio and television on a regular basis.

Oftentimes during criminal trials, I would look across the table at the defendant or to the back of the courtroom at the family of the defendant and I had little to no compassion because I felt that man's justice was being served. Further, I could not conceive of ever being seated on the wrong side of the table. Admittedly, I was self-righteous as many other believers are.

I decided that after several years as a prosecuting attorney that I wanted to go into private practice and opened my office specializing in criminal defense and as a civil plaintiff's attorney.

After a few years my practice became very lucrative and afforded me and my family (wife and daughters) a very comfortable life. We were living the American materialistic dream with the homes, cars, jewelry, wardrobe, travel, etc. that accompanies this lifestyle. We had "so called" friends, attended many social events and were in regular church attendance. During this time, I recognized God's call on my life and began studying for the ministry and serving as an associate pastor.

The aspiration of most lawyers is to one day sit as a judge and I was no exception. Still in my 30's and having served as a part time appointed judge along with my private practice for a number of years, I decided to run for a full time judgeship. I promised God that if elected, I would intensify my ministerial studies and would bring a much needed spiritual witness to the bench.

In 1981, I was elected to the bench, the first African American in this city, and began serving a six year term in January of 1982. I was the trial and administrative judge of my court with a staff of clerks, bailiffs, probation officers, secretaries and other court personnel. At this time I could not conceive of life being any better. I had, as far as I was concerned, it all.

I developed a reputation of being tough on crime. I felt that this persona was necessary to maintain a law and order respect in my jurisdiction. Non-law abiding individuals would oftentimes go out of their way not to be apprehended in my area and having to appear before me.

In looking down from the bench at the defendants who came before me I never thought I could one day be in a similar position.

Life nevertheless has its twists and turns and several years into my judgeship I learned that I was under federal and state investigation for receiving kickbacks from contractors working for the city wherein I was the sitting judge. Once favored by newspaper articles, they turned negative and hostile. Fellow lawyers and judges would see me and turn the other way. Ministers and other Believers began to avoid me and I started to feel as though I was an outcast.

I was indicted by federal and state grand juries in 1984 and was facing 132 years of incarceration. After a three-week trial in 1985, I was convicted and sentenced to 10 years federal and 12 years state to run concurrently. It was as though my life had come to an end ministerially, professionally, and materially. I had disappointed so many, mostly my family, in that I was the first in my family to attend college and professional school.

On December 5, 1985 I was required to report to federal prison in Big Spring, Texas, over 1500 miles from my family In Ohio and was assigned the prison number 31850-060. Upon arriving at the institution, I observed the doormat with the wording, Federal Bureau of Prisons – U. S. Justice Department. I reflected on the fact that I started my professional career with Justice as a trial attorney and that I had fallen from the top of the judicial system to the lowest level of society. A sad day it was.

While at Big Spring I met men (fellow inmates) from all walks of life; doctors, teachers, bankers, businessmen, pilots, ministers, professional athletes, farmers who never thought it could happen to them as I never thought it could happen to me.

I finally decided to inquire of God what happened and the Spirit of God revealed to me that there are laws of life that he has established that I had operated on the negative side of these laws and I was receiving a corresponding harvest. The Spirit of God further revealed to me that he would teach me these laws of life that I would have to develop from Genesis to Revelations whereas I would later be able to teach the laws to the Body of Christ.

It was also revealed to me by the Spirit that upon acknowledging my sin, and repenting that God would reverse my captivity and restore me for His glory.

As a result of God's mercy, after 40 months, I was paroled from federal custody but I still had remaining approximately 5 years on the concurrent state charge. So, upon walking out of the federal gate deputy sheriffs from Ohio picked me up, brought me back to Ohio and put me in county jail in the building where I had served as an assistant district attorney. My family and I were crushed to say the least.

After a few days, I was transported to a next to maximum custody state prison number 210-204 which housed murderers, burglars, robbers and rapists, men serving life and double life sentences. Some of these men had come before me on the bench. This was to have been a death sentence for me, but God had other plans. Men who one would have assumed would have been my enemies and determined to hurt or kill me, God caused to be my friends.

I was later transferred to two other state prisons where God continued to give me favor with staff and inmates and I continued to develop the laws of life series.

There came a point in time when I began to wonder if I would ever be released. The Spirit of God then impressed upon me that I should dismiss any pending appeals and rely on Him for deliverance. I. reluctantly obeyed and after 7 years of incarceration the state parole board reversed itself and granted me parole to become effective in April 1993.

Approximately a week before my parole date a prison uprising erupted and all the inmates in the state were on lockdown. But on April 16, 1993, despite the lockdown, I walked out, for when God says it is your time no man can stop it.

I returned home and God has been restoring me ever the since my release in 1993 by keeping my family intact (my then wife is now with the Lord but God has given me another Christian wife), allowing me to continue with the completion of approximately 50 books and a DVD series on the laws of life, to appear on numerous Christian radio and TV programs, to speak to various groups nationally and internationally, to testify before a congressional subcommittee in Washington, D.C., and to minister the gospel of Jesus Christ as an ordained minister in prisons and wherever doors are open.

I have the dubious distinction of being the only individual who has been a federal and state prosecutor, criminal defense attorney and civil plaintiff attorney, civil plaintiff and defendant, judge, federal and state inmate, and federal and state parolee.

God has made it all work together for my good according to Romans 8:28.

My most recent endeavor is as executive producer and presiding judge of Laws of Life Court T.V. This is a forum where individuals (Believers and non-believers) who have a controversy can bring their dispute to Laws of Life Court and receive a decision based upon one or more laws of life which are all Bible based. Also, my wife and I executive produce and co-host Laws of Life Forum where laws of life are applied to current and historical events.

I continue to receive God's favor and am working to accomplish assignments given to me. What Satan meant for evil, God has turned for good.

50 LAWS OF LIFE

ORDER FORM

$22.99
+ $5.50 SHIPPING FEE

CALL LOCAL:

www.anotherchanceglobalmedia.org

Another Chance Global Media
P.O. Box 92
Lafayette, TN 37083

PAYMENT OPTIONS:

Send check or money order to:

Another Chance Global Media
P.O. Box 92
Lafayette, TN 37083

Please indicate book name and quantity.

Name: _____   Number: _____

Email: _____

Mailing Address: _____

Book Order: _____
_____

TOTAL: _____

COMING SOON

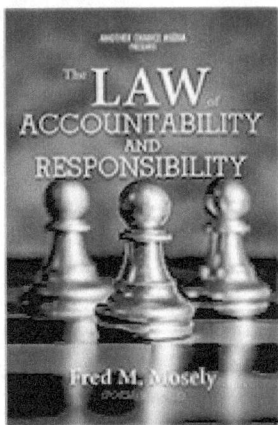
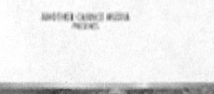

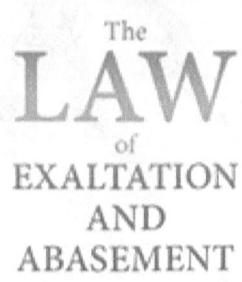

View our website for release dates: anotherchancemedia.org

www.ingramcontent.com/pod-product-compliance
Lightning Source LLC
Chambersburg PA
CBHW020355170426
43200CB00005B/184